Health Financing Without Deficits

Health Financing Without Deficits

Reform That Sidesteps Political Gridlock

Philip J. Romero and Randy S. Miller

BEP BUSINESS EXPERT PRESS

Health Financing Without Deficits: Reform That Sidesteps Political Gridlock

First published in 2016 by
Business Expert Press, LLC
222 East 46th Street, New York, NY 10017
www.businessexpertpress.com

ISBN-13: 978-1-63157-546-4 (paperback)
ISBN-13: 978-1-63157-547-1 (e-book)

Business Expert Press Economics Collection

Collection ISSN: 2163-761X (print)
Collection ISSN: 2163-7628 (electronic)

Cover and interior design by Exeter Premedia Services Private Ltd., Chennai, India

First edition: 2016

10 9 8 7 6 5 4 3 2 1

Printed in the United States of America.

Abstract

America's health system has been a polarizing issue in most presidential campaigns in our lifetimes. It is hardly surprising that an industry that consumes nearly one in every five dollars spent in the U.S. economy has loomed over our politics. Its only competition in the last few decades was the nuclear standoff with the Soviet Union during the Cold War. It will be prominent again in 2016 and beyond.

This book will guide you through the fusillade of charges, and promises, you will hear in political campaigns about health care and "reform." They will occur now that the fiscal calamity of Boomer retirement is no longer a threat: it is here. For all the attention Social Security receives, Medicare is the truly scary entitlement program, with unfunded liabilities many times larger.

This book also offers a powerful tool of reform. The Health Insurance Revenue Bond™ (HIRB) is a new and completely self-liquidating financing approach that fully funds escalating liabilities such as health care—without deficits. *If you can't bend the curve on health costs, bend the curve on the cost of funding™.* The HIRB program can assist governments in developed nations to begin the long and painful process of deleveraging.

Keywords

2016 campaign, ACA, Affordable Care Act, bending the cost curve, bond, deficit, deleveraging, financing, health care, health finance, health policy, health reform, health security, HIRB, inflation, liabilities, Medicaid, medical inflation, Medicare, municipal bond, OPEBs, other post employment benefits, pensions, politics, post retirement benefits, presidential campaign, revenue bond, states

Contents

Acknowledgments

Randy S. Miller: The one person, far more than anyone and to whom I owe everything is Claire Fransel-Miller, my spouse for 37 years. I am forever indebted, thankful, and grateful for all she has done. It has and is an extremely difficult and long journey beyond description and which few would ever endure. I married a truly remarkable woman.

Phil Romero: My formative experience in health policy came in the late 1990s when I served as executive director of the California state task force that overhauled HMO regulation, and I am grateful to my many teachers, including chairman Alain Enthoven and the 30 task force members. All cultures have special jargon and idiosyncrasies, health policy perhaps more so. I appreciated their patient help in teaching me the ropes.

For this book, we thank several reviewers who took time to offer us detailed comments. My ever-understanding spouse, Lita Flores-Romero, not only offered a very helpful scrub, but tolerated my near-complete absence for much of 2015 while I was sequestered, writing and editing. I am also grateful to Brian and Ann Nickerson, who let me impose on friendship to provide the perspective of smart people who are far outside of the health care and public finance priesthood.

Any errors herein are the responsibility of the authors, not our many teachers and supporters.

Introduction

A Political Perennial

America's health system has been a polarizing issue in most presidential campaigns in our lifetimes. It is hardly surprising that an industry that consumes nearly one in every five dollars spent in the U.S. economy has loomed over our politics. Its only competition in the past few decades was the nuclear standoff with the Soviet Union during the Cold War. It will be prominent again in 2016.

This book will guide you through the fusillade of charges, and promises, you will hear in political campaigns about health care and "reform." It will be especially noteworthy in 2016 when Republicans will remind us of Hillary Clinton's history as an aborted reformer in the early 1990s. It will also be the first election where the fiscal calamity of Boomer retirement is no longer a threat—it is actually here. For all the attention Social Security receives, Medicare is the truly scary entitlement program, with unfunded liabilities many times larger.

Former Senator Sam Nunn said that "today's problems were yesterday's solutions," and nowhere is that more true than in health policy. For most of a century, perceived problems have begotten policies that have accreted more and different problems. Throughout, American health care has grown more expensive and produced inferior outcomes. Not only are we not getting our money's worth: often more money seems to produce less health.

The intractable challenge of health reform is largely one of problem definition. Like the blind scholars describing the elephant, each ideology perceives the health system from its own myopic perspective. Liberals view the tens of millions of people without health insurance as a moral outrage. Always suspicious of markets, they believe that taxpayers should pay for what individuals and their employers do not. This follows a century-long tradition of government expansion of benefit programs.

In contrast, conservatives have never met a market they did not like. They see market competition is the ultimate protector of consumers. Conservatives believe it can perform this function as well for health care as it has in other industries.

Ideological purism can be comical, as when signs at Tea Party rallies warned: "Don't Let Government Touch My Medicare."

The purpose of this book is to help you make sense of health reform claims. You will be hearing them often in the election campaign. But if political gridlock persists—as we expect—this book also offers a wholly different approach to financing health care that is compatible with a spectrum of policy architectures, from socialized medicine to a purely market-based system. We believe that the states will be the laboratories of positive change, as they have been throughout American history, so our explanation and illustrations will be in the context of the adoption of our approach by a state.

The role of health reform in current election will be like in others, only more so. This is because fiscal realities have been ignored for decades, deferred through borrow (leverage). But we now live in a deleveraging world. Cans have been kicked down the road to its limit. Use whatever cliché strikes your fancy: The end of the road has arrived; the chickens have come home to roost; the bubble has burst. In all cases this election comes at a time when deleveraging is imperative. Health care must help solve, not exacerbate, the financial challenges of Washington DC and most states and cities.

Part I of the book explains why health reform is imperative: It is a vampire draining the life force from capitalism. Health costs are by far the largest driver of America's formerly looming, now arrived "entitlements crisis." Examine closely any public policy area and you will see health care's shadow looming over it. It is keeping tax rates high and strangling economic growth; siphoning defense budget dollars away from modern weapons for our troops; and exacerbating income inequality by stinting of financial aid from low income would-be college students. But many of the underlying forces are not unique to the United States: They pervade the developed world.

Part II puts our present challenges, and politics, into historical perspective. Health reform is a hardy political perennial, figuring in presidential politics for 100 years. Past "solutions" have often led to new problems—problems that shape electoral politics today.

Parts III and IV are a guide to the main challenges, often ignored in partisan proposals. These are the realities that face any honest politician, and all thinking voters.

Part V is a wholly different approach to financing health care. It leverages rapidly escalating health-care costs to engineer financing that is sustainable. High health inflation need not be the enemy—in fact, the faster costs rise, the *stronger* the system's finances can be. These chapters are the most technical, because we intend them to be an instruction manual for state treasurers and legislators. This system can be implemented under any policy regime: single payer, employer-based, or state health exchange. Our illustrations use states because we believe they are the hope for public innovation, bypassing an ossified Washington, DC.

Part VI synthesizes what came before to identify elements of health reform that liberals and conservatives can get behind that will actually be constructive, rather than merely symbolic.

This book was completed in late 2015, as the presidential campaign was building speed. By the time you read this, many candidates will have dropped out of the race. But their ideas may still shape policy, in the campaign and in later legislation. Some details herein will undoubtedly have been overtaken by events by the time you read this, but the basic outlines of the policy debate have endured for a century.

The Obamacare debate monopolized health policy discussions for most of a decade—the last decade available before the demographic tidal wave arrived. Realism is an overdue prerequisite to true progress on health reform. This book offers you a perspective, and tools, for your involvement in 2016 and beyond.

PART I

The Economy's Vampire: Health Care

"The path to fiscal responsibility must run directly through health care."
—Peter Orszag
Director, U.S. Office of Management and Budget (OMB), 2009

These chapters will outline the magnitude of health care's challenge to American prosperity; dissect the drivers of escalating health spending; and put the American experience in a global context. This background will motivate a discussion of reasonable goals of reform and criteria for judging any reform proposal.

CHAPTER 1

Health Care, Deficits, and the Economy

That the U.S. government, and most states and cities, are under serious fiscal challenge is hardly news. Our earlier book *Your Macroeconomic Edge: Investing Strategies for the Post-Recession World* (2011) explored this at length, with an extensive discussion of how individuals' retirement portfolios must change to protect against the coming fiscal reckoning.

The fiscal crisis is really a health-care crisis. According to the Congressional Budget Office, federal health expenditures per capita have risen at about twice the rate of incomes per capita for the past 40 years. By 2040 three health programs alone—Medicare (for seniors), Medicaid (for the indigent), and Children's Health Insurance Program—will require expenditures as a fraction of gross domestic product (GDP) nearly as large as the historical average for the *entire* federal government: roughly 17 to 18 percent of GDP. And, as noted earlier, federal spending on health-care accounts for about half of total health spending. Health care presently absorbs nearly one in five of every dollar spent in the economy, and is likely to exceed one in four in the foreseeable future.

Health Care and the States

Health care's role in the fiscal dilemma facing states and cities is even more dramatic. Most subnational governments subsidize health care not only of their employees and families but also of their retired employees. In principle, these costs are met through contributions of employees and their government employers, invested by pension funds such as CalPERS. States and cities have long failed to contribute enough to meet projected expenses; most government pension funds have significant unfunded liabilities. (In other words, projected contributions plus investment returns will not be enough to meet projected expenditures.) Unfunded liabilities at the state- and local-level total several trillion dollars. Again, the driving force is health care.

Your Macroeconomic Edge focused on the implications of fiscal problems for individual investors, arguing that the days of double-digit stock market returns would soon be over, dragged down by high taxes to pay high government debt. Five years later, that future is here.

The Only Options

Governments that have made unfulfillable promises to constituents can square the circle in only one of three ways:

- *Cut program expenditures.* Planned cost of living escalators may be suspended. Eligibility rules may be tightened up, such as the scheduled increase in the full retirement age for Social Security. This is least attractive politically because beneficiaries (senior citizens for Medicare; unionized public employees for pensions) are well organized and vote in large numbers. The programs in question often are their largest income source, or pay for their largest expense.
- *Raise taxes.* Legislatures will raise tax rates in order to meet rising expenditure obligations. This may be disguised as an attack on income inequality. However, it is an economic fact of life that activities which are highly taxed are avoided. For income taxes—the main source of revenue for most states, and the largest source for the federal government—that means higher taxes will lead to less income producing activity—that is, a slower growing economy. Governments may tax other activities, such as imposing a sales tax on services, or enforcing fines and penalties much more vigorously. Examples of this were common among strapped cities during the recession, tragically brought to light by violence in Ferguson, Missouri, in 2014.

- *Print money.* Unsustainable debt burdens can become tractable if inflation erodes the value of those debts. The central bank can expand the money supply, probably in the name of antirecession monetary stimulus. As with any other commodity, too many dollars lowers the value—the purchasing power—of each dollar. While households experience this as inflation, government earns a windfall. Income taxes that have not been indexed to inflation will rise as taxpayers' nominal income rises (even if their real income adjusted for inflation hasn't budged, or has fallen backward).

The specific mix among these bad choices depends on politics more than economics. In *Your Macroeconomic Edge*, we argued that legislatures generally lack the stomach for expenditure cuts. Instead, they will try raising tax rates. When that fails to produce the expected revenue, politicians will covertly press the Federal Reserve to expand the money supply and monetize government debt. While the resulting inflation will undermine millions of households on fixed incomes, it will bail out the politicians themselves (at least temporarily) by inflating away the debt.

The main difference between federal and state challenges is that states cannot exercise the money printing option. States do not control their currency: the national central bank (the Fed) does. As a member of the Euro zone, Greece no longer has a national currency, so it has sacrificed the ability to inflate its debt away—at least, until the widely anticipated "Grexit" from the euro.

U.S. national debt today stands at almost $20 trillion. Debt held by the public approaches 100 percent of GDP. Unfunded federal liabilities are at least five times higher. By far, the greatest contributor to this calamity is health-care inflation.

Whatever your personal interest in public affairs—for example, education, energy, environmental protection, transportation, or national defense—health care is crowding all of it out. If like some tax cutters, instead you simply want to shrink government to a size that can be drowned in the bathtub, health care again stands in the way. The attention that health reform will receive in future election cycles is not at all misplaced.

Effects on the Private Economy

For the most part, health spending saps the economy of vitality. Dollars spent by employers on health care aren't available for modernization. So, health inflation leads to less innovation, and eventually to anemic productivity growth, the key engine of economic progress.

In addition, significant economic research has demonstrated that the first source of extra health-care dollars is employees' wages. This is an unrecognized source of the growing income inequality that has dominated economic discussions in recent years, including in the 2016 campaign. Higher costs oblige employers to direct compensation increases to benefits rather than wages. Labor costs rise, but employees' cash incomes do not. Median incomes have hardly gained ground for a generation.

As can be seen, many of the salient economic issues of the early 21st century, which will define each election, are shaped by health-care spending. The stakes in health reform can't be overstated.

CHAPTER 2

The Absent Free Market

Elections are not only about personalities: They are also about political philosophies. Many elections' undercurrent is an ideological debate about the proper role of government.

A fundamental premise of the American economic system is that free markets support democracy. Competition among producers, and freedom of choice among consumers, generally promotes the public welfare. Firms which abuse their customers will lose market share to competitors that treat them better. States or cities that abuse their citizens will see residents vote with their feet and emigrate to greener pastures.

The free market is far from perfect. It is hardly "fair." The prosperous have far more options than the poor do. Democracy can become one dollar, one vote. Consumers may not always experience the full effects of their choices. There may be what economists term "externalities": impacts of my purchase on third parties. Externalities can be negative or positive. The power plant that burns coal to power my TV spews pollution into the troposphere: a negative externality. The college education I earned allows me to make a higher salary, which I spend at local merchants, expanding their incomes: a positive externality. But a vibrant market of robust competition can achieve many "public" goals. Many political debates are ultimately about how necessary government intervention is. Said differently: Can the market alone achieve our purpose?

Liberals and conservative reflexively line up on opposite sides of this divide. But the answer really depends on how closely the actual market resembles the competitive ideal. Each side holds an inbred assumption of guilt or innocence.

Our default assumption is that markets do a better job than governments for achieving a variety of desirable ends, including efficiency, prosperity, and freedom of conscience. But we part with our fellow conservatives who have never met a market they didn't like. Some industries are far too concentrated to be truly competitive. Sometimes the concentration is unavoidable. For a century, utilities have experienced such profound economies of scale (where larger firms are more efficient) that their natural state was extreme concentration. The production technology created "natural monopolies." (Today as electricity production technology is evolving such as with solar panels on building rooftops, challenging the permanence of these monopolies.)

Sometimes concentrated market power is man-made. A later chapter will argue that several features of today's health-care sector violate free market tenets. We call it the "health cartel."

Health reform is at a clear crossroads. On one side are advocates of greater government involvement, exemplified by Senator Bernie Sanders' promotion of single payer health financing. Their opponents see five decades of expanding government funding of health care (going back to Medicare in 1965) as destructive, and advocate rolling it back. Several Grand Old Party (GOP) presidential candidates wish to repeal the most recent incursion by government, the Affordable Care Act (Obamacare), whether or not they have a developed replacement.

To gain perspective on this, central debate for the 2016 campaign requires a clear-eyed appraisal of how much competition really exists in American health care. The answer is: Only in pockets. Where patients spend their own funds on procedures not covered by insurance, such as LASIK eye surgery, or cosmetic surgery, competition is fierce and delivers its customary results: rapidly falling prices and improving quality. But for the bloated, subsidized majority of the system, competition is scant. This is taken up in Chapter 11 on the health cartel.

The cartel is not some evil capitalist conspiracy but is a natural outgrowth of government policies whose unintended side effects have overwhelmed good intentions. Many reform proposals, including a number discussed in Part II, are highly incremental. They make modest improvements but leave in place the dysfunctional core.

Liberals who recommend an expanded government role have a responsibility to defend its performance thus far, and should explain why we should expect improvement.

Conservatives who wish the opposite must demonstrate how competition can provide far more pervasive benefits than at present.

We have considerable sympathy with the conservative position, but our mission in this book is to help you be a skeptical consumer (voter). Health reform will be prominent in the 2016 election, and likely in almost every future election. Some education now will help you to distinguish the candidates with real solutions from those offering only pleasant placebos.

CHAPTER 3

The Economy's Vampire

In a famous 2010 *Rolling Stone* article, journalist Matt Taibbi characterized investment bank Goldman Sachs as a "great vampire squid wrapped around the face of humanity, relentlessly jamming its blood funnel into anything that smells like money." The health sector is less assertive, but it also sucks blood out of the American economy.

Health-care spending in 2014 totaled $2.8 trillion, or nearly one in every five dollars spent of U.S. gross domestic product. Just under half of that total ($1.3 trillion) is spent by the federal government—and therefore ultimately by taxpayers. $1.5 trillion is spent by private entities, including about $1 trillion by insurance companies (ultimately by employers); $300 billion in household out of pocket spending; and $200 billion from other private sources.

In rough terms, the United States spends about twice as large a share of its economy on health care as the average of other developed nations. Health outcomes are not remotely twice as good. In fact, if a Martian examined the relationship between different nations' health-care spending per capita and health outcomes they could reasonably infer that health-care spending has negative productivity—higher spending seems to lead to worse health. Its pattern is similar to spending on K-12 education: states that spend more dollars per student often have poorer test scores.

Because of system dysfunctions discussed in Part III, health-care spending is like John Wanamaker's view of spending on advertising: Half of it is wasted—but he wasn't sure which half. Unquestionably, medicine and medical technology has lengthened many lives—average lifespans continue to climb by about a year every decade. But many countries which spend far less have longer lifespans and lower incidence of a variety of bellwether illnesses, including infant and child mortality, obesity, and heart disease. Compared to preindustrial times, undoubtedly health spending has been a lifegiver and a productivity enhancer. But this is far less obvious when America's system is compared with other systems today.

Wasted health dollars have the same economic impact as any other waste: They divert scarce resources from productive to unproductive use. Defenders commonly point out that jobs are created in the unproductive sectors, too. What cannot be seen is the jobs uncreated because of the diversion of resources.

Resources devoted to sectors whose productivity grows quite slowly impose a particular burden on future prosperity. Health care suffers from one of the worst cases of what economist William Baumol termed "the cost disease of the service sector." Many services, especially higher-skilled services such as medicine, are performed on an artisanal basis, one patient at a time. That limits the opportunities to achieve efficiencies through high volumes, as is common in many other industries. Unless consumers curtail their demand, services will absorb an ever-higher share of societal resources. Chapter 9 will argue that like university educations, health care has essentially unlimited demand.

Medical research does produce significant innovation, which has led to the happy result of longer lifespans. Some of those innovations even cut medical costs, such as pharmaceuticals that replace the need for expensive surgeries. But numerous scholars have identified as a persistent cost driver the adoption of expensive technologies to treat and keep alive patients who were previously beyond medicine. It is difficult to argue that health care has enhanced productivity—that is, has become productive faster than the economy-wide average.

PART II

Three Generations of Reform Proposals

"Today's problems were yesterday's solution's."
—former Senator Sam Nunn (D, GA)

Health reform proposals have a century-long history. Present promises should be viewed through the lens of what has been tried, and not tried, before.

In the mid-20th century, when America had recently won World War II, the Social Security program was new and faith in the government was at historic highs, there were sustained efforts to graft a national health policy on Social Security. Franklin Roosevelt demurred, considering it a policy too far, but Harry Truman bet his presidency on it. He lost the policy fight, but kept the presidency. John F. Kennedy failed but Lyndon Johnson succeeded to enacting federally funded health care for seniors.

During the several decades of wrangling over Federally funded health care, the private system evolved. Health insurance was first offered to groups beginning in the 1920s. By World War II, large employers embraced health benefits as one of the few ways to compete for scarce labor. Our present employer-based system grew rapidly in the middle decades of the 20th century, and unions' enthusiasm for national insurance faded after they had secured coverage at the labor bargaining table.

By the late 20th century, the flaws in this system were readily apparent. So was disenchantment with government. Although a Republican president, Richard Nixon, took up the mantle of national health insurance, as did Jimmy Carter a few years later, both were criticized as insufficiently aggressive and blocked by the same potential challenger for the White House, Ted Kennedy.

But throughout long periods of government inactivity, health inflation—often as much as three times the rate of growth in overall consumer prices—pressed on American households. Health care became so expensive that to be uninsured meant being undoctored. Health reform was central to Bill Clinton's successful presidential run in 1992 and Barack Obama's in 2008. But the conservative revolution of the 1980s rendered a full-scale federalization of health care politically impossible. These reforming presidents limited themselves to expanded regulation of employers and the insurance industry, leading to an insurance mandate on individuals. Clinton's reform died stillborn in 1994. Obama's Affordable Care Act borrowed heavily from it, including a political strategy that coopted key opponents to ensure passage—and several rounds of Supreme Court litigation.

These short chapters offer a very telegraphic tour of the spotty record of health reform over the past 100 years, from the Progressive Era to Obamacare. We will skip lightly and quickly, especially over the distant past. We will expand a bit for Hillarycare in the 1990s, because its political failure informed the Obamacare do-over in the late 2000s.

Presidential candidates often fall victim to the false belief that history began only with their campaign. Health reform did not begin with the ACA. It has been a locus of political maneuvering, and has helped shape the occupant of the White House, for over a dozen presidencies.

CHAPTER 4

The New Deal and Its Progenitors

From colonial times into the 20th century, American medicine was what economists call a highly fragmented industry. Care could only be delivered within a few miles of the doctor's location. Nearly all physicians were solo practitioners. Competition was fierce, keeping prices reasonable and encouraging doctors to offer special services (like house calls) to differentiate themselves from competitors. Nineteenth-century medicine was one of the closest approximations of the economist's Nirvana, "perfect competition," as could be found on this earth. Public health was rudimentary, largely in the hands of charities. It took new diseases brought by immigrants to call forth significant resources.

But technological developments in the late 18th and 19th centuries—steam powered manufacturing and transportation (railroads), later supplanted by electrification—industrialized whole sectors. Bigness brought its own reward, as large factories and companies could produce more efficiently, outcompeting their atomized peers. Industrial accidents expanded the need for medical care. Industrial unions began bargaining for fringe benefits, including health care.

The Progressive movement was first and foremost an attempt to curb the excesses of the Industrial Revolution without sacrificing its benefits. Progressivism's most vocal champion, Theodore Roosevelt, returned to politics four years after leaving the White House in 1908 out of disenchantment with his hand-picked successor President William Howard Taft's lack of Progressive zeal. When he failed to secure the GOP nomination in 1912, Roosevelt ran as a candidate of a new third party, the Bull Moose (Progressive). A central plank of his platform was a federal program of social insurance, including health insurance.

Roosevelt of course lost the race, although he drew enough votes away from Taft to elect a Democratic progressive, Woodrow Wilson. Wilson supported the first major piece of legislation to make health insurance compulsory, the 1915 AALL (American Association for Labor Legislation) bill. The American Medical Association supported AALL bill until reversing itself in 1920.

Throughout this period, medical costs rose, especially in the severe inflation accompanying World War I. In response, the Committee on the Costs of Medical Care proposed forming doctors into medical groups to achieve scale economies like those enjoyed in many other industries. It also recommended federal encouragement of voluntary health insurance, allowing for possible state-level mandates.

The industry began changing in 1929: The market began to offer what government had not. Baylor Hospital developed the first group health plan, for Texas schoolteachers. They received up to 21 days of hospital care for a 50 cent premium per month. Note that this was a hospitalization plan, not the full medical service plans common today. In the future other hospitals imitated this approach, marketing their plans under a "blue cross" trademark.

With the searing impact of the Great Depression—about half of industrial production idled, and one in four unemployed—Marx's predicted crisis of capitalism seemed to have arrived. Franklin Roosevelt (Theodore's distant cousin) was activist and experimental by temperament. He convened a Committee on Economic Security to produce a blueprint. He endorsed its main proposals, unemployment insurance and a Social Security insurance system to provide subsistence income to the indigent elderly, and made it universal to cement broad political appeal. He demurred on its recommendation to include health insurance. The committee proposed a system run by states which would mandate participation (like unemployment insurance or Social Security), but leave each state free to decide whether to enact it. In the early flush of success of the enacted programs in 1937, another committee again proposed compulsory health insurance, but Roosevelt again demurred, feeling the sting of the 1937 recession and the rejection of his Court-packing plan.

Opposition was bipartisan, with Southern Democrats allying with Republicans, out of fear that a more assertive federal government would intrude on "states' rights," including the right to segregate along racial lines.

At the end of the 1930s, World War II intervened, and profoundly changed the industry. It also cut short Roosevelt's life. His successor Harry Truman took up the mantle of reform and used it to his political advantage.

CHAPTER 5

World War II, Tax Deductibility, and the Fair Deal

Mobilization for war evaporated the depression's unemployment overnight. First, 12 million civilians became soldiers. Next, the arsenal of democracy produced around the clock. Unemployment fell from well over 10 percent to barely 1 percent. This was paid for with massive borrowing: war mobilization is the ultimate Keynesian stimulus.

Normally, this rapid heating of an economy would bring on inflation, as buyers of anything—consumer goods, raw materials, or labor—bid prices up to secure a share of scarce commodities. But price and wage controls were emplaced to prevent this. Learning lessons from World War I, the authorities allocated shortages by rationing. This policy of choosing not to allocate through price mechanisms shortages caused by exploding demand cast a very long shadow that extended into the 21st century.

Employers with huge government contracts and impossible deadlines suddenly needed to mushroom their workforces. With civilian labor scarce due to the wartime draft, the natural tactic was to offer higher wages, but this was precluded by controls. Firms with unionized workforces already offered fringe benefits—items paid for by the firm that were not direct compensation, but raised their workers' effective wages, such as vacation time and insurance. Offering health insurance, or expanding that which already was offered, was a natural arena of labor competition. Since these were business expenses, they were deductible from the firms' income. Therefore, Uncle Sam implicitly paid part of the cost through reduced taxes. Tax deductibility was ratified by regulation in 1951 and in law a few years later. Individual health insurance policies were far less tax advantaged.

Looking to the postwar future, Roosevelt saw health care as one of the "four freedoms" to which he pledged in 1944. He did not live to see it or many of his other cherished dreams, such as the United Nations.

After the war trust in government was at an all-time high. America had beaten back a depression, vanquished totalitarianism, and emerged stronger than ever from a global holocaust. Economic growth was very strong, boosted by high postwar birthrates (the Baby Boom) and high levels of education made possible by the G.I. Bill. Several New deal innovations such as Social Security and unemployment insurance were popular. The collapse of the wartime alliance and resulting Cold War legitimized internationalism and a militant foreign policy. Although the Republicans had retaken Congress in 1946, Roosevelt's successor Harry S. Truman saw a rising tide of activism as a political advantage. He promoted a slate of domestic proposals called the "Fair Deal" (in homage to the New Deal), of which the centerpiece was national health insurance. In 1948, Truman used this plan as a club to beat the "do nothing Congress" with. It won him an upset election, but did not survive the legislative process.

By the early 1950s, the employer-based system familiar today was well launched.

CHAPTER 6

Medicare and Medicaid

Social Security was a popular program upon whose coattails rode the hopes of many other domestic proposals, including national health insurance. But the anticommunist fervor of the early Cold War and Eisenhower years quashed most domestic plans for government expansion in the late 1940s and 1950s. But by the early 1960s, the political pendulum had swung again, ideologically and generationally.

The G.I. generation elected as president one of its own for the first time in 1960. Kennedy's short tenure is better known for international matters—the botched Bay of Pigs invasion; his sober firmness that forced Soviet missiles out of Cuba; and his initiation of what later became the Americanization of war in Vietnam. But while quite conservative (by present-day Democratic standards) on foreign policy, he was original and activist in some areas of domestic policy. He was the first Democratic president to support a tax cut as a Keynesian stimulus during a slow economy (although the cut did not pass until after his assassination). He also proposed Medicare—government-funded medical care for the elderly—at the beginning of his campaign in 1959.

Senior citizens' demographic presence had expanded significantly during the century, from 4 percent of the population in 1900, to 10 percent by 1960 (continuing to about 12 percent in 2010). Seniors vote at higher rates than younger adults, even Camelot-mobilized young voters. Kennedy had watched Truman from the House of Representatives in 1948, and he saw Medicare as a potent election, and later reelection, issue in 1960 and 1964. With his death his successor Lyndon Johnson doubled down on Kennedy's initiatives and proposed the Great Society following his landslide election in 1964. Many of its components were hatched under JFK but vigorously promoted by LBJ. This program included universal care for seniors (Medicare) and for the indigent (Medicaid). In a tribute Johnson invited Truman to witness the bill signing.

The American Medical Association had opposed most federal initiatives in health policy, fearing a loss of doctors' autonomy. Its winning slogan for decades was to brand the proposal they opposed as "socialized medicine." This had worked in the Red Scare of the late teens and early 1920s, and in the early Cold War. But it failed to keep GOP opposition to Medicare united in 1965.

The late 1960s and 1970s reform debate remained focused on national health insurance. Richard Nixon proposed a narrow version in the early 1970s but was blocked by Senator Edward Kennedy's unwillingness to accept its less than universal scope. Kennedy was likely interested in preserving the issue for a 1972 presidential run, later torpedoed by Chappaquiddick. Kennedy similarly sparred with Jimmy Carter in the late 70s, possibly for the same reason. (Kennedy ran a stillborn presidential campaign in 1980.) Instead of expanded government, Nixon signed the Health Maintenance Organization (HMO) Act in 1973 that allowed the creation of "capitated" organizations that received a fixed fee per patient. The premise was that HMOs would economize care if their revenues were capped. Two decades later, the effects of these constraints provoked significant backlash, leading to the aborted Clinton health reform plan of the early 1990s.

CHAPTER 7

Hillarycare and Its Progeny

The Affordable Care Act

Health policy was a mostly a political backwater through the 1980s. Ronald Reagan's presidency was about defeating totalitarianism abroad and arresting the growth of government at home. The main exceptions were attempts to right Medicare's finances, which met such intense opposition from senior citizens that the reform law was repealed within 18 months of passage. Social Security was also partly reset to account for lengthening lifespans. Throughout, health costs continued to expand.

By 1992, health spending consumed more than one dollar in every seven of the U.S. economy. Bill Clinton won a close election by positioning himself as a centrist Democrat eager to tackle liberal sacred cows like health care. To symbolize the issue's importance, he made First Lady Hillary Rodham Clinton chair of the Administration's health reform task force. Ms. Clinton was the very public face of an effort that was generally closed to all but invited technocrats.

The Health Security Act, the plan produced in the fall of 1993, called for mandatory employer-based insurance. It significantly increased insurer regulation; for instance, it required premiums to be "community rated"—all members of a community must pay the same premium—with prohibitions on exclusions for prior conditions. Employers were mandated to offer insurance, and individuals were obliged to purchase and keep insurance.

The insurance industry saw an arrow aimed at its profit margins. It waged an intense fight against the plan, in the halls of Congress and on the airwaves, featuring the devastating TV ads in which a middle class couple, "Harry and Louise," complained about how their insurance costs would rise under the plan. The legislation stalled in the Senate and was declared dead in the Fall of 1994. The insurance industry's opposition to Hillarycare was even more potent than the American Medical Association (AMA's) stance against Medicare 30 years earlier.

Obamacare

A decade and a half later, the original energizing force for Barack Obama's 2008 candidacy was his opposition to the invasion of Iraq in 2003 and to the counterinsurgency still underway in 2007, augmented by President Bush's surge (reescalation). But the 2008 financial crisis and subsequent global recession reordered agendas profoundly. It vitalized his quixotic insurgent candidacy, trouncing Hillary Clinton (then-senator from New York), the presumed Democratic front runner. And it forced noneconomic items, including the Iraq war and health reform, off his urgent agenda in the first months of his presidency.

But Obama was obliged to offer policy conciliation to the liberal wing of the party that got him elected, so by mid-2009, health reform rose in priority. There may also have been a recognition that a Democratic Congress was a very temporary asset, which mandated quick action on a handful of long-cherished hopes—especially when economic and international realities stalled other signature initiatives, such as closing the terrorist prison at Guantanamo, or offering significant mortgage relief to millions of underwater homeowners. Beginning in late 2009 health reform began dominating the Obama Administration's domestic agenda to a similar extent as economic recovery had in the early days of his term.

The development of what came to be known as the Patient Protection and Affordable Care Act (ACA) (but more often called the ACA, or simply Obamacare) was shaped by a conscious effort to avoid the fate of Hillarycare. In practice this meant two things. First, insurers were involved intensively from the beginning—so much that critics (including us) argued that insurance companies essentially wrote the bill. Second, unlike the closed task force that developed Hillarycare, the Obama administration heavily deferred to Congress (then fully controlled by Democrats). In practice, both meant great influence by industry lobbyists.

The resulting bill was complex, and borrowed heavily from Hillarycare, but with differences that reflected 15 years of learning. Insurance coverage was again mandatory, with escalating tax penalties if violated. A modified version of community rating was adopted, with a maximum spread between premiums for the oldest and youngest members of the covered population. In practice, this meant that young members of an insured group (a community) would subsidize older members, as is true in most insured populations. To finance coverage for those of lower incomes, significant subsidies were made available through states that opted to join the program, with the federal government offering working capital to participating states for the first few years. Medicaid eligibility was expanded to households earning up to 400 percent of the poverty level.

Key Hillarycare opponents were coopted under Obamacare. The mandate meant that insurers got a guaranteed market expansion, paid for by taxpayer funds. They were also offered a profit floor, concealed as a minimum "medical loss ratio"—the proportion of revenues paid out in claims. Free market proponents distrusted the insurance mandate (although it had been proposed or enacted by several Republican governors including Mitt Romney of Massachusetts and Arnold Schwarzenegger of California), but welcomed the bills call for "exchanges" in which insurance companies would compete. (Many states hosted only a very few insurers—a highly consolidated industry.)

The opponents left in the cold were "single payer" advocates. These were the 21st century analogs to national health insurance supporters of the early and mid-20th century. They argued that government-run systems were significantly more efficient. (This debate is taken up in Chapter 17.) In the latter stages of Congressional debate they pushed for a "public option"—allowing onto the menu in a given state the option of a state-funded program.

The ACA became law in March 2010. Opposition in Congress was intense, and the bill narrowly passed on a party line vote. It galvanized opponents, giving birth to the Tea Party and the Republican takeover of the House of Representatives in the 2010 elections. However, Democrats maintained control of the Senate, blocking GOP efforts at repeal. (The

GOP would not retake the Senate until 2014.) Efforts to overturn the ACA moved to the courts, but the U.S. Supreme Court has (controversially) upheld the constitutionality of key provisions, in 2012 and again in 2015.

Early indications of the actual effects of the ACA are decidedly mixed. The ranks of the uninsured have dropped significantly—by about 10 million, varying by source of the estimate. This is seen by supporters as a major victory, especially in light of major problems with the enrollment process when the ACA website was launched. Opponents argue that it is difficult to imagine otherwise, given a federal mandate and expansion of Medicaid subsidies. More significantly, the rate of increase in health-care spending slowed in the early years after ACA enactment. Advocates gave Obamacare credit, while critics attributed it to other causes such as a slow economy, with support from the Congressional Budget Office. According to the Organization of Economic Cooperation and Development (OECD), this deceleration is occurring throughout the developed world, so it isn't attributable to any specific national policy. Health-care demand may be constrained by modest income growth.

Clearly health reform is a story with many chapters. Some have yet to be written. The 2016 election will in part be a ratification—or a renunciation—of the ACA and the party that brought it into law.

PART III

What Is Wrong With Democratic and Republican Plans

These chapters identify broad themes or patterns in the proposals that originate in each ideological camp, to identify their Achilles' heels. Democratic proposals rely on nationalization to replace a competitive market—or as in the ACA, delegation to an oligopolistic insurance industry. GOP proposals assume a degree of competition that does not really exist.

After setting the stage with an overview of health policy in the 2016 presidential campaign, several chapters outline realities about the American health system that are ignored in reform plans.

Even if Obamacare defenders manage to change the subject and keep it off center stage in 2016, several deadlines baked into the ACA guarantee it will become highly salient in the 2018 elections.

CHAPTER 8

2016 Plans

Health reform is almost certain to be a defining issue in the 2016 election: in the presidential race, and in many down-ticket contests. Republicans took control of the House of Representatives in 2010, and added the Senate in 2014, largely on the strength of their opposition to the Affordable Care Act (ACA). Many Democratic congressional candidates are staking their candidacy on a vigorous defense of the ACA. The nominal Democratic front runner, former Secretary of State Hillary Clinton, made her first mark on national policy in her chairmanship of the health reform task force that produced the Health Security Act in 1993.

Democratic candidates like Clinton, Vermont Senator Bernie Sanders, and former Maryland governor Martin O'Malley are positioning their message around the declining economic fortunes of the middle class, known to economists as income inequality. This can have great resonance with a wide swath of voters (beyond the Democratic base) because the broad facts are on their side. Median incomes have indeed slipped backwards for several decades. Once this problem was confined to blue-collar occupations, but it now is common among college graduates also.

Many Democratic candidates see an attack on income inequality as compatible with a defense of the ACA. We disagree. As this book has stressed, mandated benefits that are part of the ACA (as they have been of most Democratic health reforms of the past century) expand health care costs. If coupled with mandated coverage by employers, as the ACA does like the Health Security Act (Hillarycare) from which it sprang, this increases labor costs. Employers have shifted labor expense from wages to benefits. This is one of the primary causes of stagnant incomes.

Republican proposals are characterized by Democrats as being strictly negative—repeal the ACA, without offering a specific alternative. For months following the 2014 elections, this was fair point. Competitors in the crowded GOP field limited their exposure to attack by keeping their statements quite general. But inevitably candidates began differentiating themselves with concrete proposals. Louisiana governor Bobby Jindal, who began his career as a senior state health official, offered a plan in April 2014, long before declaring his candidacy. Others followed: as of this writing in October 2015, former Florida governor Jeb Bush, Wisconsin governor Scott Walker, and Florida senator Marco Rubio have published position papers. Several others have expressed strong personal views but have not presented proposals, including pediatric neurosurgeon Ben Carson and Kentucky senator Rand Paul (an ophthalmologist), as well as Texas senator Ted Cruz. For several of these, the facile criticism—they are against the ACA, but what do they propose?—is not unreasonable. Even many of the formal "plans" are thin on detail, as is common in a campaign.

At first glance, it may seem surprising that the Democratic candidate with significant health policy experience, Hillary Clinton, has been so mute about health reform in the present campaign. In her senatorial reelection campaign in 2006, she was outspoken in presenting expansive opinions on a range of health policy issues. She also did not shrink from health issues in her 2008 presidential campaign. Along the way she partnered with former House Speaker Newt Gingrich, a longtime antagonist, to advocate for initiatives to digitize patient medical records and make them portable. But in the present campaign her statements have been limited to a strong defense of the ACA. This may be a tactical retreat, to minimize vulnerability to GOP criticism; many Republican candidates are also following this conventional political wisdom, as noted.

It may also be an effort to protect her left flank. Her most potent challenger at this writing is Vermont senator Bernie Sanders, a socialist running in the Democratic campaign. Income inequality and attacks on plutocracy are the core of his campaign, but on health policy he is the only serious candidate advocating a single payer system.

Another reason why health reform has not been a major theme of the Democratic race is that cost pressures seemed to be abating for the past few years. ACA supporters attributed the moderation of health inflation to the new law, while opponents attributed it to a slow economy during and after the 2008 to 2009 recession. Health was expected to recede in voter saliency. But, by mid-2015, insurers had begun announcing proposed premium increases for the following year, which are well into the double digit range—at a time when general price inflation (the Consumer Price Index) is negligible. This issue is likely to become significant again in early 2016.

In the early stages of a fluid campaign, any attempt to summarize the positions of the candidates is bound to quickly become obsolete. (For that matter, the slate of candidate will change as some leave the race and others enter late.) The following table captures their positions as of Sept. 2015. The "ACA" entries are for reference. Plans for candidates who may leave the race during the early primaries are preserved here because elements of their plans may be taken up by other candidates, or used in future legislation.

Question marks indicate candidates who have not specified their position on the topic as of Sept. 2015, reflecting only our inferences about their views.

Role of government

National health care or single payer	Employer-based w/regulation	Mainly private
	ACA	
Bernie Sanders	Hillary Clinton 2004	Jeb Bush
		Ted Cruz?
		Rand Paul?

Tax treatment

Favor employers	Equalize	Favor individuals
ACA	Jeb Bush	
	Bobby Jindal	
	Scott Walker	

Mandated coverage

Individual	Employer	None
ACA	ACA	Ted Cruz?
Hillary Clinton 2004	Hillary Clinton 2004	Rand Paul?
		Scott Walker
		Bobby Jindal

Insurance regulations, for example, prohibition of exclusions for prior conditions; profit ceilings

Heavy	Light	None
ACA	Jeb Bush	
Hillary Clinton 1993		

Cost and spending containment

Government regulation	Managed competition	Market pricing
	Hillary Clinton 2004	Scott Walker
		Bobby Jindal

Transparency and technology enhancements

Significant	Minor	None
	ACA	
	Hillary Clinton 2004	

PART IV

The Key Problems in American Health Policy

CHAPTER 9

Problem I—Unlimited Demand Due to Third Party Payment

Suppose that you are in an automobile dealership shopping for a car. You want a sturdy, no frills, and economical model. After all, every dollar that you must spend on the car, now and in the future, comes out of your pocket, so value is important. Besides the overhelpful salesmen, you have many other information sources available: customer ratings from *Consumer Reports* and review websites; five-year cost of ownership from Edmunds; and comparative prices from many competitors' sites, among many others.

Now consider an alternative. You are in the same showroom, but you know that someone else will pay between 85 and 100 percent of the cost of the car: both the initial purchase price, plus ongoing maintenance. This is just as well, because prices are not posted. And you have only rudimentary information about each car's performance and quality. So you cannot judge value. But you have no reason to try, since most of the bill is paid by someone else.

Would you be as frugal and value-conscious in the second scenario as you were in the first?

Welcome to the first prevailing problem with the American healthcare system: third party payment. For decades the vast majority of the cost of health services—the actual bills tendered by doctors, hospitals, and labs—has been paid through intermediaries, mainly private insurers. Those insurers receive regular premium payments that are mostly paid not by patients, but by their employers. Only a minority of total health spending came directly from final consumers (patients): the remainder came either from their insurers (who are contracted by employers), or from governments.

Third-party payment fundamentally distorts the market for health services. When the consumer making a purchase decision is not the same as the party paying for that decision, the rationing function that prices play in most markets is absent. Since health care is necessary to stay alive, there would be near-unlimited demand for it without the constraining force of prices.

The situation is similar to the market for higher education services (colleges and universities). A bachelor's degree is widely seen as a prerequisite for entry into the middle class. So, demand for college is effectively limitless. To the degree that it is financed with loans, the end consumers (students) are temporarily shielded from the cost of their purchase decision. (They will feel the full effects later, when they leave school—with or without a degree and a job—and are obligated to pay the loans back.)

Not surprisingly, in the face of rapacious demand, suppliers—universities and doctors—have unfettered pricing power. The prices of both higher education and health services have risen at more than three times the Consumer Price Index for decades. The crowding out of other worthy activities by escalating prices, emphasized in Chapter 3, is not unique to health care.

In theory market, competition should moderate price inflation. Some firms will underprice their competitors to gain market share. But price competition is a far less effective business strategy when the consumer is (mostly) not spending their own money. They may be only 10 or 15 percent (common copay percentages) as price sensitive than if every dollar spent was their own.

Problems on the demand side of the market aren't the only ones. Competition is also stifled on the supply side, as discussed in Chapter 11. The absence of effective competition has led many on the left to advocate renouncing the market entirely in favor of taxpayer-paid health care. The broader issues associated with government run or merely government-financed (aka "single payer") systems will be discussed at length in other chapters. For now we will only note that regardless of the system, if patients do not pay for a significant share of their health costs, they will not be price sensitive, and demand will grow boundlessly. *Without prices to ration demand, some alternative means of rationing will be necessary.* (This is the "death panels" issue beloved by Obamacare opponents.) All health systems ration demand: the question is whether that rationing involves patients in the decision, or not.

This may all seem very abstract if the decision involves life-saving care in an emergency: no patient will shop around in a crisis. But only a small part of health spending is for urgent situations. A far larger portion is for chronic conditions and routine care. As a result of the momentum of history, American health "insurance" performs far more than only traditional insurance functions: financial protection in crisis situations. It is as if your car insurance covered gasoline purchases, oil changes, and routine inspections. Employer-based, hyper-broad health "insurance" has been a foundation stone of America's health-care problem.

As we will discuss in Chapter 18, if employer health coverage cannot be eliminated entirely, it could be limited to true catastrophic coverage, paying only very large claims for treatment of the most serious conditions. This is not mere theory: It exists already, known as high deductible health plans. Premiums are far lower than traditional health insurance, so patients are responsible for a large share of the cost of their care. These plans have been one of the first significant moderating influences on employer health benefits costs in many years. According to a study in *Health Affairs*, wider uptake of such plans could reduce health spending by $57 billion, even if annual deductibles were as low as $1,000—lower than in many traditional plans. Not surprisingly, firms are offering attractive incentives to encourage their employees to sign up for them. It is also not a surprise that employees have rapidly taken up high deductible plans, with enrollments rising from well under one million to 14.5 million by mid-2015. Incentives still matter—when the consumer's own money is on the line.

CHAPTER 10

Problem II—High Costs = Poor Access

Health-care policy debates resemble the parable of the blind scholars and the elephant: Each touches a different body part and comes to a different conclusion about the animal before them.

Liberals note the tragedy of tens of millions lacking health insurance, driving many of them to get care only sporadically (leaving many chronic conditions untreated), and in the most expensive way: hospital emergency rooms. Liberals often define health reform solely as improving access to care. Generally, they wish to replace the employer-based system at least partially with taxpayer-subsidized insurance. This was the core of Obamacare.

Conservatives note the metastatic growth in health costs that has obliged employers to devote all new labor dollars to benefits and none to wages. This has stopped the economic progress of the middle class in its tracks and aggravated income inequality. Even more worrisome for the future, company funds spent on rising benefits (especially, for an aging workforce) are unavailable for investments that maintain competitiveness. So, America's health system has become a severe handicap to U.S. companies competing in world markets. Some industries are so weighed down by health benefit costs that their companies' CEOs—hardly statists— have publicly endorsed a larger government role as a competitive imperative to offload company health costs.

With larger market share for government has come expanded mandates as to what constitutes minimally "acceptable" coverage. Requirements that insurers cover contraceptives, mental health treatment, and gender reassignment surgery have become part of the policy agenda, first at the state level, and now in federal legislation such as the Affordable Care Act. Requirements that procedures be covered, and paid for by premiums, have long been a problem at the state level: in 2010, 2,156 mandates were in state laws. Over the past generation, the most coherent policy prescriptions, and most of the enacted reform legislation, has come from liberals: conservatives have mostly fought a losing retrograde campaign against expanding government intervention. (Some of the premises of the conservative position are factually wrong, as discussed in the next chapter.)

Rarely is the logical relationship between liberal and conservative positions acknowledged. Expanded coverage mandates aggravate the health access challenge by making insurance more expensive. Many lower and even middle-income workers have no need for the mandated services, but they are obliged to subsidize them through their insurance premiums. Young and healthy workers often opt out of health insurance, which raises the insured population's risk level, requiring escalating premiums. So well-intentioned political efforts to make insurance more generous for those who have it prices those who don't out of the market.

Expanded government-funded health "insurance" that goes far beyond traditional insurance functions almost guarantees high prices: because patients are not spending their own money; and because mandates can spark an insurance "death spiral," where insurers' price increases push less risky patients out of the insurance pool, raising costs (and therefore premiums) for those who remain.

Many liberal health reforms may aggravate rather than solve America's health system crisis. An expanded government financing role such as "single payer" simply duplicates, and magnifies, the third party payer problems mentioned in the previous chapter. Increased subsidies may extend "access"—coverage—to many previously uninsured: about 10 million have been newly covered under Obamacare (ignoring those previously insured who switched to subsidized insurance). But instead of controlling costs, more coverage without system changes will only aggravate health inflation. And with an expanded government role, more health decisions will be made by legislatures and thus be political, not medical.

The conservative response—less government and more competition—omits some important realities, however correct it is in theory. That is the subject of the next chapter.

CHAPTER 11

Problem III—The Health Cartel

When Gandhi was asked his opinion of Western civilization he responded, *"I think it would be a good idea."* Clear-eyed observers of the American health system with a fondness for free markets should say the same about competition in health care: It would be a good idea.

Liberal and conservative debates over health system design have centered on the role of government; or said another way, the degree to which competition delivers in health care the same benefits as in other industries. Many conservatives take this as a matter of free market religious faith. We have no quarrel with this view as a theoretical proposition, but we see only spotty evidence of real competition in practice.

This chapter describes the health system, component by component, by comparing real conditions to those in two different market structures you learned about in Econ 101: "perfect competition" and "cartels." We will argue that at present we face a health cartel—and one that is becoming progressively *less* competitive.

A Refresher on Competition and Cartels

Every beginning microeconomics student is introduced to a theoretical construct: *perfect competition.* "Perfect competition" is to economists what a perfect vacuum is to physicists: an idealized representation of a simple system (sometimes called a model) to make its main elements easy to understand. Once the ideal is understood, we can introduce messy real-world complications to make the model more realistic and useful.

The main assumptions of perfect competition are:

- *Highly dispersed market power.* There are many separate firms competing against each other, for many separate customers. No one actor can significantly affect the market price. Economists consider these firms as price "takers."
- *Commodity offerings*: Customers cannot distinguish among the products and services being offered by different competitors, except by their price.
- *Ease of comparison*: Customers can compare alternatives readily. The product or service is not so complicated or opaque that they stay loyal to a brand out of risk aversion.
- *No differentiation*: Because firms cannot differentiate their product (e.g., they cannot associate special qualities with their brand that would allow them to charge a premium), all competition is based solely on price.

This produces an economist's (and conservative's) utopia. Intense price competition assures that consumers get the lowest price possible, and the best treatment. Poorly treated customers have plenty of alternative suppliers to which they can take their custom. Firms produce efficiently and charge just enough to eke out a meager living.

Conservatives have never met a market they didn't like. If all markets were like this, they would be right. But every firm would dearly love to *evade* competition entirely: If they could they'd escape the perfect competition's profits prison. One way to evade competition is to lobby government for special treatment; several examples of this occur throughout this book. Another way is to consolidate the many firms in the industry down to far fewer. Economists call industries with only a few competitors an "oligopoly." If members of an oligopoly collude (collaborate with one another), such as agreeing not to reduce prices below a minimum threshold, the oligopoly is a *cartel*.

Although cartels are illegal under the national competition laws in most advanced economies, cross-border cartels are not unknown. A prominent example is Organization of Petroleum Exporting Countries (OPEC), the Organization of Oil Exporting Countries, an association of the governments of oil-rich nations. OPEC attempts to coordinate (and sometimes limit) members' production to keep oil prices within a target range.

A simple measure of market concentration is the sum of the market shares of the top few firms; four is the number most commonly used. Four firm concentration ratios (the sum of the top four firms' sales divided by total industry sales—that is, the sum of the top four firms' market shares) of 10 or 20 percent indicate a highly fragmented industry; but 80 or 90 percent reaches oligopoly or cartel levels.

The siren song of cartels is powerful, so much that Adam Smith warned against the inclination of businessmen to form a "conspiracy against the public or in some other contrivance to raise prices." Often the collusion is subtle, such as monitoring competitors' prices to match any changes (made far easier by computers). We will use the term "cartel" loosely here with a meaning closer to the classic oligopoly.

Cartel Behavior in American Health Care

Restraint of competition—that is, cartel behavior—is rife throughout the American health system. The next few sections outline how far many parts of the system deviate from perfect competition.

Providers

On the surface, health-care providers seem highly fragmented, as close to perfect competition as almost any industry. There are hundreds of thousands of doctors nationwide, many still organized in small offices and clinics.

However, medical care is mostly a local service, so market shares within small geographies matter more than national shares. In many cities a large fraction of specialists affiliate with only a handful of medical groups. In many metropolitan areas there is only a single hospital, or at most two. A handful of hospital chains control many of the beds nationwide. The economies of scale that have consolidated many other local service industries such as newspapers—most largish cities have a single daily paper—are similarly consolidating hospitals. In the late 20th century, medical groups and hospital chains consolidated to regain bargaining power versus insurers, which had begun consolidating half a decade earlier.

Milton Friedman pointed out over 50 years ago that medicine, like many other licensed professions, has captured state licensing boards. These boards are notorious for restricting entry into the profession, while turning a blind eye to malfeasance by those already licensed. Actions performed in the name of patient protection mainly keep fees high.

Insurers

The Affordable Care Act (ACA) was passed in 2010 with significant insurance industry support. As mentioned in Chapter 7, this was a stark contrast to the insurers' 1994 "Harry and Louise" attack ads that sank Hillarycare. The Obama White House assiduously cultivated insurers to neutralize them, and the prospect of tens of millions of new customers paid for with taxpayer dollars was attractive.

But in the summer of 2015, observers began questioning if there was an additional quid pro quo. In rapid succession, two major health insurers made merger offers for competitors: Anthem for Humana, and Aetna for Cigna. Speculation raged that the firms had received assurances of leniency from antitrust authorities, in contrast to the recent Federal Communications Commission (FCC) veto of Comcast's attempted acquisition of Time Warner Cable and Sysco's blocked acquisition of U.S. Foods, or the stringent conditions placed on the American Airlines and U.S. Air merger.

Insurers have also succeeded in prohibiting competition across state lines. They have taken a page from the 20th-century regulatory capture playbook of banks, who successfully blocked interstate branching until the late 1970s. Not surprisingly, some of the fiercest overt opponents of interstate insurance competition are state insurance commissioners.

By any reasonable standard, health insurance is already a highly consolidated industry, with insurers holding far more market power than any employer customer. Government nonchalance may be payback for insurers' cooperation in Congress to pass the ACA.

Immediate Customers (Employer Purchasers)

Although there have been some successful attempts at starting employer purchasing cooperatives to counterbalance the power of insurers, in general the customer side of the health insurance market is far more fragmented than the insurer side. Increasingly trade associations and business-oriented nonprofits are attempting to level the playing field, but power is still weighted far more to insurers. State-level exchanges are beginning to bring some market power to customers in the individual market, which is even more fragmented. Note that because insurance is not portable when the insured changes jobs, individual employees have no effective leverage over insurers, regardless of the size of their employer.

Government

By definition, government-financed health care is a *monopsony*—a market with a single customer. In theory it should be able to negotiate attractive prices with the vendors it uses—pharmaceutical companies, health-care providers, and insurers. In many instances, it achieves this. But being inherently political, government does not always act in its own best interest as the payer of more than 50 percent of all health-care dollars. Medicare's Part D, for example, is prohibited by law—that is, by Congress—from negotiating volume discounts for pharmaceuticals. A reasonable inference is that pharma lobbyists persuaded Congress to rein in the Medicare program's power as a monopsony customer.

Patients

As in most markets, in health care the final consumers (patients) have the least power. Not only are they by definition completely dispersed, but several other factors conspire to inhibit them from seriously comparing among providers or insurers.

As mentioned earlier, patients are largely spending other peoples' money—government's if the patient is old (Medicare) or poor (Medicaid); otherwise the funds of the insurer with whom their employer contracted. Patients have limited choice among insurers, since they are constrained by the options their employer has chosen. Many medical procedures are too urgent to allow for any real comparison shopping among providers, and consumers lack price information anyway. Even for nonemergent situations, such as chronic illnesses, serious comparisons are nearly impossible. There is little comparative information on provider effectiveness widely available—no equivalent of *Consumer Reports* for doctors—and even if there were, very few providers offer *ex ante* pricing information. Business practices among providers still reflect the "someone else pays" model.

Under Obamacare, government-midwifed insurance purchasing marketplaces and cooperatives off individual consumers the ability to enjoy the bargaining power of groups. These were innovated in as a number of precursor state programs, and also contemplated under Hillarycare. Early ACA results suggest there has been considerable adverse selections (uptake by especially unhealthy individuals), overwhelming premium income and leading to the dissolution of several state coops.

Overall

Conservatives fighting to the death to "preserve competition" need to take a clear-eyed look at the industry. Obamacare has begun several salutary reforms, such as encouraging the digitization of medical records that will ease the migration of dissatisfied customers and allow for greater pricing transparency and facilitating (subsidizing) state exchanges. But the industry's practices in general are still premised on the "spare no expense; do not question the doctor" model of the mid-20th century.

Ideologues can draw either of two polar opposite conclusions from this chapter.

Liberals, who are generally deeply suspicious of markets in any case, will see the preceding as vindication that a private sector-based health system is a fantasy: They believe the only viable alternative is a government-run, or at least government-paid ("single payer") system.

Conservatives will argue this is all the result of prior misguided policies, and repealing Obamacare is a necessary first step. However, you may wait a long time for them to explain the second step.

A sensible health system design must take these realities into account. That is the goal of Parts V and VI.

CHAPTER 12

Obamacare

Hillarycare 2.0

As noted, the most recent major reform was of course the Patient Protection and Affordable Care Act, more commonly known as the "Affordable care Act" (ACA), or colloquially, Obamacare. The ACA was passed by Congress in the late winter of 2010 and signed by President Obama in March 2010.

Obamacare was outlined in Chapter 7, but like other 1,000-plus page legislation, it contains many pieces that cannot be neatly summarized. Some of its main provisions include:

1. Health insurance access was significantly expanded by mandating employer coverage for all full time employees working for firms with headcounts of 50 or more.

2. For others, federal subsidies were expanded, to include households earning up to 400 percent of the poverty level. The primary mechanism was an expansion of Medicaid, a federally-subsidized, state-administered program. States received full subsidies to encourage their participation, reducing to 90 percent in 2016. About 30 states opted to participate in one form or another.

3. Insurers are required to cover all applicants: applications cannot be denied due to preexisting medical conditions. A version of community rating is required, where customers with similar demographic characteristics must be charged the same premiums.

4. To keep a lid on the risk pool, all individuals are mandated to purchase insurance. They face tax penalties enforced by the IRS for failure to do so—minor in the early years, rising later.

5. Insurers are offered "risk corridors," where their costs are capped. If they incur costs above the cap, they are paid from a reinsurer funded with pooled revenues from all insurers, and where necessary, from government funds. (In 2015 Congress appropriated less than required, which drove several insurers from the market.)

6. A variety of incentives are offered to induce health-care providers to modernize their practices, including digitization of medical records, payment for outcomes rather than for services, and bundling of payments.

The focus of Administration spin and media coverage of Obamacare's implementation in its early years was on expanding insurance coverage. As of mid-2015 the number of uninsured had been reduced by about one fourth: from 45 million to roughly 32 million nationwide. This accomplishment was hardly unblemished: The launch of enrollment websites was fraught with technical problems, for the federal system and for some states such as Oregon. Such challenges seem to be unavoidable in large government information systems.

Many critics question the significance of this coverage expansion. They argue that it would be strange if coverage did *not* expand with insurance purchase mandated and the price of health care greatly reduced for many through subsidies. In terms of the challenges described in the three previous chapters, Obamacare used a frontal assault—government subsidies—to improve insurance coverage. It preserves the employer-based insurance system. It avoided many of Hillarycare's political vulnerabilities by preemptively conceding to insurers several core elements. Insurers did not oppose a government mandate to add tens of millions of new customers, paid with taxpayer funds.

But on the other two core challenges—unlimited demand sparked by third party payment, and an uncompetitive health system (cartel)—Obamacare largely is silent. Arguably it has exacerbated these challenges. Patient dollars are a reduced share of total spending, so the third party payer problem is worse. And in several areas, especially insurance industry consolidation, the cartel has strengthened.

In fairness, many of the smaller scale reforms, such as record digitization and outcome-based payment, will take years to bear fruit. It is inaccurate to judge Obamacare a complete failure, as many Republican advocates of repeal have done.

A fair criticism of Obamacare would be that in the name of passing *something*, its proponents plucked the lowest hanging fruit—subsidized coverage expansion—rather than the most significant problems. By preserving the third party payment system, Obamacare left the demand side of health care untouched. And for all advocates' talk about "bending the cost curve" (downward), the microeconomic reforms, while steps in the right direction, are very small steps.

But when reforms seem to see passage only once every several decades, it is hard to argue that the ACA's modest results have been worthy of their historic opportunity.

CHAPTER 13

The Shadow of 2018

If the 2016 election is not the defining moment we expect for health reform, 2018 may force the issue.

Learning an important lesson from the legislative failure of Hillary-care, the drafters of the Affordable Care Act (ACA) phased in early many of its most popular features, such as its Medicaid subsidies to states, and allowing adult children to remain on their parents' insurance well into their 20s. It back-loaded the necessary price to keep the bill close to deficit neutrality, which was a political imperative. These bills start coming due in the second half of the 2010 decade.

The element that has received the most political attention is the "Cadillac tax." In order to raise the added revenue necessary to cover the ACA's cost, several new or expanded taxes were incorporated. Some, like a surtax on investment income, had no particular relationship to health care. Others, like a tax on medical devices and on especially generous insurance plans, arguably had some health policy rationale. This last mentioned became known as the "Cadillac tax."

A basic theme of this book has been that consumers who are shielded from the economic impact of their choices make worse choices. Over the decades, many labor unions have negotiated generous benefits packages for their members, with employees responsible for minimal premiums or deductibles. Many companies have offered similar perks to their executives. The Cadillac tax imposes a surcharge on plans whose costs exceed a threshold, roughly $10,000 per covered individual. Its primary goal was revenue-raising, but a side effect is to discourage such destructive plans. The tax, which is not deductible as a company expense, enters into force in 2018.

Unfortunately, this denial of employer tax deductibility, although a step in the right direction, applies to all employer health expenses above the threshold—including employer incentives for employees to enroll in high deductible plans. Likewise, small employers who offer employees stipends in lieu of insurance cannot deduct the cost of above-threshold stipends.

As mentioned, the largest group of insured individuals who will be subject to the Cadillac tax are union members, a core Democratic constituency. This has led to jockeying among Democratic presidential candidates who are generally stalwart supporters of the ACA, like Hillary Clinton, to propose the tax's abolition. This may be an area of rare bipartisanship: a suspension of the tax is being mooted in Congress as we write. But repeal of the tax without a replacement policy will have two deleterious effects. It will raise the ACA's long-term cost significantly, and it will remove a valuable prod toward greater consumer exposure to the consequences of their decisions.

The ACA has so many parts that it is likely more hidden problems will be found in coming years. But since the bitter medicine (taxes and restrictions) was delayed and the sweet subsidies were front-loaded, these problems are surfacing in political circles only slowly. For those that do not gain traction by the 2016 election, they will present a campaign opportunity for congressional candidates running in 2018.

PART V

A NonPartisan Health Financing Alternative: HIRB®

By Randy S. Miller

These chapters will outline an approach to finance health liabilities, implementable at the state level: a municipal revenue bond, HIRB™. Part V was written by HIRB's inventor Randy S. Miller.

The final chapter of this section will illustrate the range of policy regimes in which HIRB can be used, and comment on how it compares to major proposals and policies that are currently prominent (or likely to become so in the next few election cycles).

CHAPTER 14

Bending the Curve on Funding Health-Care Cost

"You never change things by fighting the existing reality. To change something, build a new model, which makes the existing model obsolete."

—Buckminster Fuller
1895–1983
Architect, Systems Theorist, Author, Designer and Inventor

In June 2015, the U.S. Supreme Court rendered a second major decision affirming the constitutionality of the Patient Protection and Affordable Care Act (ACA) more commonly known as "Obamacare." For the second time, the ACA has withstood significant and substantive judicial review.

Our purpose is focused on the financing and funding aspects for providing health-care services promulgating a new model called "Health Insurance Revenue Bonds" or its acronym "HIRB" program.

Part V advocates a new paradigm for how both the nation as well as the individual States can approach matters of public finance. This is especially significant when you consider the present amount of outstanding public debt at both the federal and state level. It is common knowledge; the last thing our country, the States (as well as other nations) need is further exacerbating the increasing principal amount of debt outstanding.[1] HIRB *does not* contribute toward increasing the principal amount of financial debt obligations or unfunded benefit liabilities outstanding. The HIRB program is designed to reduce the cost of funding such obligations and has consistently demonstrated, under variable conservative parameters the ability to achieve that exactly.

This new paradigm we call HIRB introduces an innovative and quite counterintuitive strategic financial management methodology for public financings. Upon initial review, the HIRB models may appear to not make any financial sense. Nonetheless, the HIRB model holds up. The mathematical computations are rock solid and there has been substantial multidisciplinary due diligence conducted over a period of years (actuarial, accounting, legal, economic and fiscal, finance and banking and two select senior state budget officials). The HIRB approach may be applicable to financing other public endeavors, as discussed briefly later. Our focus is on the financing and funding of health-care benefit liabilities—more precisely "health financing."

Leveraging Assets Versus Leveraging Liabilities

Anyone who has ever used a mortgage to purchase a home or other real estate asset has employed leverage.

Consider two alternative scenarios:

1. You purchase an asset such as real estate property for $100,000. If you purchase it with $100,000 of your own money then sell the asset for $110,000, you have realized $10,000 gain representing a 10 percent return on your money; or
2. You purchase the same asset for $100,000. You use $20,000 of your own money and obtain a mortgage for the balance of $80,000. You sell the asset for $110,000. Out of the $110,000 proceeds, $80,000 pays off the mortgage and $20,000 is the return of your investment principal. The balance of $10,000 is the realized capital gain, representing a 50 percent investment return on your original $20,000 equity investment.

Quite a significant difference in your favor: a 10 percent return versus a 50 percent return. That is the power of leverage.

Leverage magnifies positive investment returns—by five times in this example. Unfortunately, it also magnifies losses. In the aforementioned scenario 2, even a mere 20 percent decline in the price of the asset would wipe out your equity. But assuming a rising underlying trend in the asset's price, the lower the investment principal (i.e., the higher the degree of leverage), the greater the investment rate of return is leveraged.

Sir Issac Newton's third law in physics states: "For every action there is an equal and opposite reaction." This raised the question: *If you can leverage an asset, then why not leverage a liability?* The mystery was how. If leveraging an appreciating asset means you put in as little of your own money as possible, then the answer to leveraging a rising liability must be to put in more money. One of the keys to this puzzle was in figuring exactly how the new money is determined, designed, and managed. This was something far easier said than done. It took approximately three years of research and development to figure out the puzzle.

In every other borrowing transaction of any kind, the total cost of the financing transaction is the amount of interest paid for the borrowing. With the HIRB program, the total cost of funding the project is *less than* the amount of total funded expenditures in health-care costs paid and in fact, may offer a potential for gains. For both public and private sector expenditures such as health care, the real substantive and compelling promise of the HIRB program is stabilizing the financial outlay for a rapidly rising liability. This can make health financing more affordable and sustainable.

HIRB is a serious substantive measure for health reform. Liberals will be satisfied because HIRB brings financial stability and integrity for the benefits promised or obtained. Conservatives will be satisfied since the HIRB program costs less to fund than present methods without reliance on stinting providers or patients, businesses, or government.

The HIRB program cannot solve every challenge in American health care, but it does allow policy to sidestep many of the most contentious debates that have blocked effective solutions for decades.

If you can't bend the curve on health-care cost, then bend the curve on the cost of funding™. This can be the exact result of the HIRB program. HIRB is a financing approach that originated not on Wall Street but on Main Street—in Eugene, Oregon.

CHAPTER 15

Financing Basics

Revenue Bond Financings

Bonds, regardless of type or class, are financial instruments that are evidence of debt, a category of liability. In public finance, there are fundamentally two kinds of bonds: General Obligation Bonds (G.O.s) and Revenue Bonds.

G.O.s are secured by the full faith, credit, and taxing power of the bond issuer, commonly a state or political subdivision. The proceeds from the sale of the G.O. bonds may be used for any lawful purpose, as defined by state law.

Revenue Bonds are issued to finance a specific public purpose project that will generate income from one or more sources. The security for the Revenue Bonds is the pledge of the income stream generated by the use of the project.

The laws of the State in which the project is domiciled governs the statutory authority to issue revenue bonds; the kind of projects that may be financed and the procedures and processes to be complied with to issue the revenue bonds. Commonly, capital projects are "bricks and mortar" projects. They are tangible and they have a determined useful life. Useful life generally means how long the project will last before it has to be substantially replaced.

Under the Revenue Bond structure, the state government establishes a nonprofit public corporate entity (the "Entity") that serves as the financing conduit and specifically in the context of the HIRB program, operates the funding mechanism for the Project. It serves four basic purposes on the project:

1. To issue the revenue bonds;
2. To oversee construction, operation, maintenance and management of the project;

3. To repay the principal and interest due on the revenue bonds issued; and

4. To charge user fees sufficient to operate and maintain the project.

Fees charged to those who use the project are charged under the provision of a rate covenant. This covenant or promise is contained in a trust indenture, which is a written contract between the Entity, as the Bond Issuer; and a Trustee, representing the interests of the bondholders. Thus, the cost of these public purpose projects are paid for and shared by and among the users of the product or services provided by the project. This means the cost of the project is ratable over its useful life.

The term of the Revenue Bonds and the periodic payments (called amortization) of principal and interest payable (called debt service) to the bondholders must remain within the useful life of the project financed with the bond proceeds. Therefore, Revenue Bonds are generally considered self-liquidating debt and are not charged against the debt limitations or debt ceilings established under the laws of the state in which the Entity and the project reside.

Insurance Financings

Insurance is a form of financing. The very fundamental concept of any kind of insurance is based upon all members of the risk pool sharing the financial consequences of a covered risk event occurring to any one member of the pool.

In the context of insurance financing basically, each member of the risk pool sells off a risk exposure to a party (typically an insurer). By selling the risk to the insurer, the consideration the member purchases heavily discounted dollars (payable under the terms and conditions of the policy contract) guaranteed for future delivery if—and only if—a covered risk event occurs. Depending upon the nature of the risk, it may never occur (e.g., fire insurance on real property, whereby the insured property may never experience a fire). The claim proceeds paid to the policy beneficiary (or his or her assignee) are discounted future dollars purchased with a relatively small periodic monetary contribution called "premiums."

If the health benefit plan is insured, the liability to the purchaser (the obligor of the promise to provide a financial benefit) of an insurance policy contract is the premium. If the health benefit plan is self-insured or self-funded, the liability is the cost of claims plus the cost of operating the benefit plan. Under either financing arrangement, the total cost includes the cost of claims plus administrative cost. "Retention" refers to that portion of premium kept by insurer to cover operating expenses, profit, risk, and pooling charges. Mutual insurers do not per se charge a profit though will have a margin built into the risk charge that is added to their surplus. An insurer's surplus is the percentage amount of its assets in excess of those needed to meet the insurer's outstanding obligations—its precautionary reserve, or cushion.

There are two key differences between an insurance financing versus other types of financings: the pooling aspect; and the fact that an insurance policy contract, as a financial instrument, matures upon the occurrence of an event, such as illness or injury, whereas other financial instruments (e.g., such as a Revenue bond; G.O. bond or a bank CD) mature as a function of time.

In the context of risk pooling, the cost of funding is actuarially determined by the dollar cost of a claim and the expected frequency of claims. Primarily, an insurance company creates the risk pool and operates the benefit plan. However, the insurance company does not assume any risk and instead employs an underwriting quality control process. With a stock-owned insurer, their objective is no different than any other commercial enterprise to keep operating costs as low as possible and to maximize shareholder or owner profits. With a mutual insurer, its policyholders are the owners of the insurer. Thus, with a mutual insurer any and all profits inure to its policyholders; there are no stockholders.

Traditionally, an insurance company provides principally two functions: an administrative function (they process claims) and a banking function (they cut a check to the beneficiary or the beneficiary's assignee such as the doctor or hospital). Each member of the risk pool pays a periodic contribution or premium, as defined under the terms and conditions in the insurance policy contract.

From the health insurer's perspective, claims are inevitable. The larger the risk pool, statistically, the more predictable the risk of claims the lower the per capita cost to fund the risk pool for the benefit of members. For decades the economics of health care have been dominated by risk and cost shifting among providers, insurers and employers: cherry-picking low risk patients or discouraging high risk ones. Under the Affordable Care Act (ACA) this shifting can be to taxpayers. However individually rational these behaviors have been for system actors, they have resulted in high friction and administrative costs, and are the opposite of public policy goals.

Prior to the enactment of the ACA, for several generations the United States has had a severely fragmented health financing structure based upon market competition for those who can afford to pay, along with heavily subsidized public programs such as Medicare and Medicaid for eligible populations. Rates of medical inflation well above those in the rest of the developed world call into question the degree of real competition in the American system. The failure of competition to deliver the quality and productivity benefits it has achieved in other industries has led to an economic, fiscal, and moral crisis. One reason market competition amongst health insurance *plans* does not work is that commercial insurers *do not* take risk. They only pool risk and administer or operate the benefit plan. They will collect whatever amount the health claims cost is over a stated period of time, plus plan administration costs.

Competition in health care may occur amongst health care providers of products or services or both, including though not limited to hospitals, doctors, medical laboratories, clinics, manufacturers and distributors of medical supplies and durable equipment, and so on. In principle, competition should be based on value delivered: improvements in health outcomes per dollar. However, in the present American system comparative quality information is scarce and pricing information almost nonexistent. Patients rely on insurance companies to screen providers, but many insurers (lacking quality information) focus exclusively on price. This has vitiated competition based on value.

For most (not all) goods and services, customers are price-sensitive, so higher priced offerings enjoy less demand. For some items—education, some professional services, or health care—customers assume price indicates quality, because they cannot appraise quality directly. So higher prices can stimulate demand rather than depress it.

To put it another way: Competition and insurance financing are fundamentally antithetical. Competition is by definition adversarial, and customer switching creates friction. Risk pooling is inherently aggregating, based on treating large populations identically.

Analogy for HIRB: Life Insurance

Individuals and organizations, such as governments facing a future of predictably growing liabilities, such as health care costs can address them one of two ways: The conventional approach is to allocate a rising income stream to match the expenses or reduce future promises, such as anticipated liabilities. An alternative is to prefund the liabilities by generating a stock of capital sufficient to meet the expense stream—especially if that stream can be lowered through some structural or operational changes.

As an analogy, consider a 40-year old who has a long-term need for life insurance. Typically, in the early years the need for the life insurance is for income replacement purposes. Later in life, the need may shift or change but the need for having life insurance doesn't diminish or disappear; it only changes; for example, business or personal liquidity or highly efficient financing for estate tax and administration costs.

Fundamentally, there are only two means to approach this from an insurance financing perspective. One plan is to purchase term insurance for each year during one's lifetime. Term insurance premiums escalate as the insured individual's risk of death increases with increasing age. The second approach would be to purchase permanent life insurance (e.g., whole life, universal life, or variable life). Initially, a permanent insurance has a higher cost in order to start accumulating a stock of capital that can eventually pay rising mortality expenses. Likewise, the refinance of a mortgage into a lower rate mortgage requires new capital to pay off the original liability stream in a lump sum.

Instead of life insurance, consider any range of rising government liabilities being generated by unstoppable demographic forces such as aging: health-care deferred maintenance and pensions. Any changes in the liability structure for example, health reform will likely require new capital to prefund the reform(s) in a lump sum. HIRB's approach allows new debt instruments to be floated to generate that prefunded capital *without* premise of accruing or exacerbating a public budget deficit and may possibly realize net gain.

Historically, the conventional means of health financing use the "pay as you go" strategy. This is comparable to purchasing term (temporary) life insurance. Our alternative approach is comparable to purchasing permanent insurance that has long-term sustainability. All other things being equal our alternative approach (HIRB program) cost less to fund the same liability.

CHAPTER 16

HIRB and Public Policy

HIRB is compatible with a range of public policy architectures for health systems. This section attempts to stay above ideological arguments and describe the sweep of possible policy regimes.

In 2006, The International Bank for Reconstruction and Development/The World Bank published a study entitled "Health Financing Revisited—A Practitioner's Guide." In the study, the authors state:

> *"Risk pooling is the collection and management of financial resources so that large unpredictable individual financial risk becomes predictable and is distributed among all members of the pool."*[1]

The World Bank promulgates three fundamental principles of public finance:

1. Raise enough revenue to provide individuals with a basic package of essential health-care services, which provide financial protection against catastrophic medical expenses caused by illness and injury in an equitable, efficient and sustainable manner.
2. Manage these revenues to pool health risks equitably and efficiently.
3. Ensure the purchase of health services in ways that are allocatively and technically efficient.[2]

In large measure, the "health financing arena" in the United States has not followed these principles. It can be argued that the Affordable Care Act (ACA), at best, is retrograde; ceding more, not less, power to health insurers. At nearly $3 trillion, the United States "health financing arena" collects and spends more than enough revenue to meet the needs of the risk pool. However, revenues are not managed equitably or efficiently, so they do not ensure the purchase of health-care services in an allocatively or technically efficient manner.

> *"Risk pooling and prepayment are critical for providing financial protection ... There are various ways for governments to finance public health insurance programs and each should be assessed on the basis of equity, efficiency, sustainability, administrative feasibility and administrative costs ... Governments should strive to reduce fragmentation ... to lower administrative costs and provide basis for more effective risk pooling and purchasing."[3]*

> *"Large proposed increases in public health spending must be considered in the context of the available fiscal space – the budgetary room that allows a government to provide resources for a desired purpose ... . Governments can create fiscal space ... borrowing resources, either domestically or from external sources."[4]*

In its study, the World Bank presents four risk pooling or spreading mechanisms[5]

1. A government funded national health service system (Single Payer universal health care)
2. Social health insurance
3. Voluntary or private health insurance; and
4. Community-based health insurance

A national health-service style system has three dominant features:

- Funding primary comes from general revenues;
- It provides medical coverage to the entire population; and
- Services are delivered through a network of public providers.

These features give a national health service the potential to be equitable and efficient, at least in theory. *Risks are broadly pooled without the dangers of adverse selection common in more fragmented systems.* Unlike other systems, it relies on a broad base of revenue sources. However, when power is decentralized or shared with local authorities, decision making may become convoluted and uncoordinated.

Social health insurance systems are characterized by independent or quasi-independent insurance funds with a reliance on mandated payroll contributions from individuals and employers. *These include a clear link between the earmarked contributions and a defined package of health-care benefits.* The insurance funds are generally nonprofit though supervised by government. Sometime there may be multiple funds whose mechanisms compensate for different risks across funds, such as through reinsurance.

Community-based health insurance plans were *precursors to many other social insurance programs.* "They may be broadly defined as a non-profit prepayment plan for health care controlled by a community that has voluntary membership." Switzerland is one example whereby the purchase of private insurance is mandated by law. This is the core of the ACA. Note that Switzerland is very different demographically, politically and culturally, from the United States.

Private or voluntary health insurance coverage *supplements the publically funded coverage especially in high-income countries.* Private insurance is purely a discretionary purchase paid for with private funds.

Reducing the cost of health care comes down to two basic options:

- Providers reduce their fees or compensation, or
- The way health care is financed and funded changes

Financing reform is the only means of spending control that avoids major surgery on the practice of medical care.

ACA is one possible context within which the HIRB program can operate. ACA presents the establishment of a business partnership of the federal government, numerous state governments and the health insurance industry (cartel), created and enforced under sanctions of federal law and significantly subsidized by the taxpayer. We do not think it is possible to restructure health financing in the United States without the use of subsidies to some extent or without the engagement of the health insurance industry. Subsidies are unavoidable due to stagnant inflation-adjusted wages for the mass of population over the past several decades. Financing is unavoidable—neither the federal or state governments are in present fiscal condition to undertake added obligations to provide schedules of benefits to added populations (tens of millions of uninsured).

Nonetheless, such a close legal arrangement by and among government and industry is uncommon in American history, but not unprecedented. One example of an earlier close relationship may be the development of the railroads in the 1800s. The federal government granted the land rights for the private development of the railroads.

Each of the major industries within the health sector has been consolidating for several decades. Hospital mergers in the 1990s and 2000s responded to insurer mergers. At the time of this writing, the dominant players in the health insurance industry are again concentrating by acquisition or merger. There are several pending transactions in process. If these proposed monopolistic mergers and acquisitions are not blocked by either the USDOJ or the courts, our nation will have only a handful of suprainsurers within the entire country. Considering that competition does not work to reduce health-care costs, the latter result may be a few huge for-profit commercial enterprises operating as de facto monopolies controlling the spending allocations equal to about 17 to 18 percent of the national gross domestic product. Thus, the health insurance industry (cartel) ("AHIP" = America's Health Insurance Plans, the industry's lobby in Washington, DC), will have its customer base guaranteed under federal law along with a profit margin of up to 20 percent of every premium dollar expended in a nearly $3 trillion dollar market of which more than 50 percent is funded by taxpayers. So, political fights over the need to "preserve competition" are disingenuous at best.

The juxtaposition clearly illustrates the compelling advantages of HIRB because HIRB costs less to fund than present conventional financing methodologies. To put this more succinctly, the HIRB program *is* the competition.

The American health-care financing "system" is a hybrid of the previous pure models. Medicare is a form of national health care for the elderly and Medicaid is a social insurance program jointly funded by the federal and state governments and administered by the States. It is debatable whether many large-scale health policy debates retain much relevance. The difference between government-paid health care and that paid by an insurance oligopoly is more semantic than substantive.

HIRB as Public Policy

HIRB is predicated upon the fact that financing for health-care services is a high budgetary priority for everyone and HIRB results need not be predicated upon changes to any health-care delivery model or schedule of benefits presently provided. The HIRB program's broad objective is to mitigate the enormous annually recurring and increasing liability called the cost of health care. It is compatible with any likely policy regime.

As public policy, HIRB is a strategic financing and financial management framework creating the fiscal space government needs to facilitate and obtain the previously stated goals and objectives.

The public policy supporting HIRB is not new. For decades, capital infrastructure projects such as school buildings, water and sewer systems, wastewater treatment facilities, power generation facilities, hospitals, airports, port facilities, toll roads and bridges, and mass transportation system infrastructure (the "projects"), all serving a public need, have been financed through the issuance of revenue bonds. This same public policy can be adopted for implementing health financing through the HIRB program.

The reasons HIRB is counterintuitive and foregoes conventional wisdom and practices in public finance and health financing is, the models illustrate substantial borrowing incurring very significant principal amounts of debt; repaying such debt with interest; adding a new stream of revenue; paying all outstanding liabilities (bonds and health care); funded and paid for all the administrative and operation expense for the HIRB program, and in the end spend less in total <u>without</u> accruing a deficit, mortgaging the future, or otherwise kicking the can down the road.

- To those who hold the view that market competition can or will reduce health-care costs (even though historically it has not)—HIRB *is* the competition.
- To those who hold the view that health care should be funded by tax revenues through government—HIRB can be applicable.
- To those who hold the view they prefer some other alternative other than the two previously stated—HIRB can be designed and meet this objective.

Under any of the three preceding comments, HIRB will cost less to fund then conventional methodologies.

If there is any one singular issue that presents the most compelling fiscal and socioeconomic problem facing the United States going forward, it is health-care spending. In our opinion and solely viewed from a financing and funding perspective, the ACA is very convoluted and for the most part centric to the commercial health insurance industry cartel—we do not view it as oriented toward the constituency it presumes to serve. The reader should not misconstrue this to mean that the ACA should be trashed lock, stock, and barrel either.

The HIRB model foregoes conventional wisdom in its construction, design, and operation. HIRB is a methodic and structured advance prefunded public financing that results in causing an "arbitrage effect." ("Arbitrage" entails exploiting differences in the price of an item at different times or in different markets.) The result of this arbitrage effect is applied toward reducing the cost of funding. Medical inflation, heavily driven by demographics and utilization, becomes a lever, not a threat and this may include the health-care liabilities incurred from Medicaid expansion under ACA. The HIRB program provides financial and fiscal sustenance to the framework of the Exchanges established under the ACA. HIRB is in no way premised on ACA. HIRB was designed well over a decade earlier.

In public finance, advance **refunding** bond issues are common. In an advance **refunding** transaction, the bond issuer issues new bonds to take advantage of a lower interest rate. This is similar to a homeowner who refinances their mortgage when interest rates drop. The proceeds from this new bond issue will pay off all the outstanding bonds from a previous bond issue carrying a higher interest cost. However, the terms upon which the outstanding bonds were issued do not permit the issuer to pay off the bonds prior to their stated maturity unless there is provision for the issuer to call in outstanding bonds prior to the scheduled bond maturity date. Therefore, in order for the issuer to take advantage of a lower interest rate, the issuer will issue the new bonds and deposit such bond proceeds in an escrow account held on behalf of the outstanding bondholders. When the redemption date arrives, the issuer calls in the outstanding bonds and use the monies in the escrow account pay the outstanding principal and interest. The result is the original bond issue is completely paid off and the issuer has refinanced such outstanding debt at lower interest expense.

An advance **pre**funding bond issue may have similarity though it is not the same. An advance **re**funding is a static transaction. An advance **pre**funding bond transaction is not static. It must be managed dynamically. An advance **pre**funding must be prospectively recalculated and recalibrated on a periodic basis and on many heretofore unrelated data points, each of which needs to be monitored and tracked. This is fundamental to the HIRB program's financial success—and therefore of its success at achieving financial stability and benefits sustainability for covered populations. HIRB achieves improved health system financial stability without sacrificing the interests of any stakeholder. The FAQ section elaborates on this bold claim.

The HIRB program is flexible (within limits). HIRB can be perpetual. In public finance terms, HIRB is both the project and the financing—the health financing is "the project." HIRB as a capital project consists not of bricks and mortar but rather of an integrated financial information management system. This essentially is the HIRB model "in motion."

The public policy underlying such project financings is simply that the users of the project should be the ones paying for it. The same rationale applies to the HIRB program. Other than for those beneficiaries who live in poverty, pay no taxes, and are subsidized (which means someone else is paying their subsidy), there is no such thing as "free health care."

During its congressional gestation, the ACA's proponents argued that competition among insurers participating in the Exchange (healthcare.gov) would bend back health-care costs. In fact, as noted earlier, with the present trend path, our nation will have only a very few major supra-health insurers administering nearly every insured health-care plan in the country. Furthermore, under fiat of federal law, the ACA has mandated a guaranteed profit margin of 15 to 20 percent of a multitrillion dollar market to the health insurance industry—about half paid by government—at a time when debt at every level of government has been rapidly increasing. This is in addition to the preexisting fiscal and budgetary pressures from unfunded liabilities particularly relating to pension and health care, estimated to be at least ten times the magnitude of explicit government debt. In other words, in its present form the ACA is a huge gift to the health insurance industry cartel very much like the way Medicare Part D (prescription drug benefits) was a huge gift to the pharmaceutical industry. Both at a time when the country can least afford it. Nonetheless, while we certainly do not guarantee it, within the context of the HIRB program, we will not be surprised if the health insurance industry or cartel saw its profitability increase.

CHAPTER 17

Why HIRB Works

HIRB has undergone extensive scrutiny and due diligence by various professionals in economics, finance, public policy, law, health care, actuarial, accounting, and a few select government officials. HIRB has malleability (within limits) such that we have a high degree of confidence in HIRB design parameters to accommodate a wide range of policy objectives.

HIRB earns interest and the amount of interest earned exceeds the amount of interest paid. Based upon our sensitivity analysis, the stress test for HIRB seems to be up to approximately 200 basis points (bps) negative spread. In the world of bond finance, this is a huge spread and is a very significant positive factor in favor of HIRB program. In every model, there is no deficit spending; no mortgaging the future; no kicking the can down the road.

The HIRB program may allow the State to reduce its Medicaid budget *without* diluting benefits. This may also apply to the Federal government expenditures relating to Medicaid (the "FFP"—Federal Financial Participation). In addition, it may be possible to keep the level or rate of contributions for private sector enterprises, local governmental units, participant contributions, or all less than the rate of medical inflation.

It is of little value to attempt to explain the minutia of exactly how HIRB works in detail. There are too many variable data points and policy questions that must be considered in how HIRB is designed for any particular population or State. It has been difficult enough for an audience grasping the model having the model laid out in front of them (fully printed on 8 × 11 paper the HIRB model rolls out 10 feet). It's been completely useless attempting to explain the "How" part by auditory without visualization. It took many such experiences until the developer of HIRB realized this "communications problem" stemmed from the fact that when presenting the HIRB model to a health-care-related professional they didn't really understand the public finance bond side very well, if at all; presenting to a public finance related professionals they didn't really fully understand the insurance aspects very well. Regardless of who was in my audience, they had limited understanding; limited to one part of the model.

What transpired from this was the realization that the HIRB program and the context in which it may operate are an amalgamation of principles of municipal finance; insurance principles; public policy and related tax and insurance law resulting in a model that meets nearly every public policy objective expressed to be achieved across the political spectrum within the context of U.S. health reform … and cost less than when compared to conventional health financing methods. The details of exactly how HIRB works is most prudently addressed and delineated with specificity in the final bond prospectus (bond offering circular) in a specific transaction along with any other required or prudent disclosures including public communication efforts.

Health financing is about financing a liability called health-care costs. In the context of health financing, the "asset" is good health and well-being and in turn, a more productive flourishing society.[1]

CHAPTER 18

HIRB's Robustness Over a Range of Interest Rates

Interest Rate Sensitivity Analysis

Each of the following three examples illustrates the summary impact of different interest rate scenarios. The numbers are from three different HIRB models. All are based upon the State of California demographic and financial profile data when HIRB was first formulated. All data used in each of these three models are identical, other than the following scenario variations:

- The first scenario uses a 3 percent bond rate and 3 percent for the earned interest rate.
- The second scenario uses 5 percent bond rate and 5 percent for the earned interest rate.
- The third scenario uses 1 percent bond rate and 0.40 bps (bps means basis points; 100 bps = 1 percent) for the earned interest rate. This is a –60 bps negative spread between the bond rate and the earned interest rate.

You will see the positive impact of higher interest rates and tolerance under low interest rates with a negative spread. Even considering "pushing the interest rate envelope" in either direction, HIRB program produces positive results financially, and therefore fiscally and economically.

Contrary to conventional wisdom and practices in *public finance*, higher interest rates are exponentially far more favorable than lower interest rates.

Contrary to conventional wisdom and practices in *health financing*, borrowing to fund health-care benefits can cost less than conventional methods of health financing.

The HIRB program is no panacea for addressing the problems with health care in the United States, but we think it's a fair imitation.

"If you can't bend the curve on health-care cost, then bend the curve on the cost of funding (TM)."

First Scenario

Interest Rate used 3 percent for bond rate and 3 percent earned interest rate.

Source of funds	Dollar amount	Allocation (%)
Federal payments	$70,980,000,000	13.17
State payments	64,545,000,000	11.97
Pvt. Sector plan sponsors	360,722,323,740	66.92
New revenue	41,443,044,878	7.69
Earned interest	1,347,998,957	0.25
Total:	$539,038,367,575	100.00

Use of funds		
Medicaid liability	$141,960,000,000	26.34
Pvt. Sector liability	396,685,576,560	73.59
Bond interest paid	359,017,814	0.07
HIRB operations expense	33,773,200	0.01
Total:	$539,038,367,574	100.00

Results

Real $ Savings	$955,207,942	Earned interest	$1,347,998,957
Operating expenses	33,773,200	Bond interest	−(359,017,814)
End balance	1		
*Net gain/(cost)	$988,981,143		$988,981,143

- Gain = 18 basis points as a percentage of total liabilities

Note: Savings to the state or federal government are not reflected in this summary.

Second Scenario

Interest Rate used 5 percent for bond rate and 5 percent earned interest rate.

Source of funds	Dollar amount	Allocation (%)
Federal payments	$70,980,000,000	13.16
State payments	64,545,000,000	11.97
Pvt. Sector plan sponsors	360,722,323,740	66.89
New revenue	40,786,136,422	7.56
Earned interest	2,249,077,778	0.42
Total:	$539,282,537,940	100.00

Use of funds		
Medicaid liability	$141,960,000,000	26.32
Pvt. Sector liability	396,685,576,560	73.56
Bond interest paid	603,188,179	0.11
HIRB operations expense	33,773,200	0.01
Total:	$539,282,537,939	100.00

Results

Real $ Savings	$1,612,116,398	Earned interest	$2,249,077,778
Operating expenses	33,773,200	Bond interest	-(603,188,179)
End balance	1		
Net gain/(Loss)	$1,645,889,599		$1,645,889,599
*Net savings/(Cost)			

- Gain = 31 basis points as a percentage of total liabilities

Note: Savings to the state or federal government are not reflected in this summary.

Third Scenario

LOW INTEREST RATES minus 0.60 percent basis points (60 bps) negative spread—using 1 percent for bond rate and 0.40 percent bps for the earned interest rate.

Source of funds	Dollar amount	Allocation (%)
Federal payments	$70,980,000,000	13.17
State payments	64,545,000,000	11.98
Pvt. Sector plan sponsors	360,722,323,740	66.95
New revenue	42,371,177,408	7.86
Earned interest	179,546,104	0.03
Total:	$538,798,047,252	100.00

Use of funds		
Medicaid liability	$141,960,000,000	26.35
Pvt. Sector liability	396,685,576,560	73.62
Bond interest paid	118,697,491	0.02
HIRB operations expense	33,773,200	0.01
Total:	$538,798,047,251	100.00

Results			
Real $ Savings	$27,075,412	Earned interest	$179,546,104
Operating expenses	33,773,200	Bond interest	(−118,697,491)
End balance	1		
*Net gain/(Cost)	$60,848,613		$60,848,613

- Gain = 1 basis point as a percentage of total liabilities

Note: Savings to the state or federal government are not reflected in this summary.

A Brief Comment

A few comments in reference to each of the three preceding "Sources and Use" summaries are given here.

The currency market is the largest unregulated market in the world. Billions in currency trade every day. In the currency trading business, the profit or loss on any particular trade is measured in "Pips"—One (1) Pip = 1/1,000 (0.0001) of one cent (0.01). Thus, what currency traders keep their eyes on is the fourth digit to the right of the decimal point of any currency pair exchange rate because this is how they measure their profits or losses on every trade. When this is applied on such a magnitude of trades, the profits or losses realized may be measured in very small fractions which can translate into substantial nominal profits. The HIRB program produces a very similar result though in a very different context. Though the savings may be measured in small fractional percentages, such fractions translate into substantial nominal dollar amounts.

The mechanisms may be different though the physics (as we previously commented near the beginning of this Part V) never changes. All that ever changes is our understanding. It is the only thing that ever does.

CHAPTER 19

A Health Insurance Requisite

Mandated Participation

The fundamental principle of any insurance financing, regardless of the nature of the risk, is to pool and spread risk over a large group of people so that all members of the pool share payment for the financial consequences of a risk event occurring to any member of the pool. This fundamental insurance financing principle makes mandated participation by all, an absolute requirement. This may collide with some ideologies, especially among conservatives. This is not a political issue. It is an issue of sound *conservative* public financial planning.

Every proposal, before and after the Affordable Care Act (ACA), regardless of source(s) has proposed new sources of revenue, defining such revenue sources in varied of ways, some direct, some indirect. Expending energy debating political philosophy and the role or size of government in the context of promulgating restructuring health financing is largely pointless. Furthermore, in 2012 the U.S. Supreme Court affirmed the constitutionality of mandated participation under Congress authority to levy tax.

Having a schedule of "tax penalties" to pay for not having health insurance coverage seems almost subterfuge to the ACA stated goals and objectives. If the tax penalty is significantly less than the health insurance policy premium in a particular year, then the tax penalty may be relatively little to incent having health insurance. This may fail to inhibit, and may even increase, adverse selection to a risk pool.

Debates about the size of government and the magnitude of taxes for health care can be largely nullified by HIRB. It all comes down to this: the cost of funding the payments for health-care services. There are two conditions are central to HIRB:

- *Universal coverage or no adverse selection*: Expenses must be predictable for the program beneficiaries as a whole. This means a large covered population. In insurance terms, there cannot be "adverse selection," where only individuals with above average risk opt in. For this reason, most health policy proposals, including the ACA, specify "universal coverage": where all members of the eligible population must participate (and pay the requisite premium).
- *High-compliance revenue collection*: Likewise, certain revenues must be assured. The employer's (as plan sponsor) relationship to the employee (as plan participant) is of little significance. What is significant and consequential is the efficacy of collective revenues, such as through payroll deductions.

Under conventional means, the cost of funding is equal to the cost of health-care payments. Under the HIRB program, the cost of funding is something *less than* the cost of health care.

CHAPTER 20

Summation

HIRB's Features and Benefits

HIRB permits a very wide range of health expenditures to be sustainably financed. Its key features include the following:

1. A ratable base including households, corporates, and governments.
2. It has the ability to absorb deferred health maintenance by patients who previously skipped treatments due to lack of access to health care services, many times due solely to costs.
3. It can substantially reduce the structural fragmentation in the "health care arena."
4. It may be designed such that health-care benefit coverage would be free and independent of employment sponsorship.
5. The HIRB program may be applicable to either a single or multiple payer design.
6. There is no deficit financing. There is no mortgaging the future. There is no kicking the can down the road.
7. Even with continued health inflation, annual funding contributions may stay flat and level or *may* increase at a rate much less than the health inflation rate.
8. HIRB program has long-term sustainability.
9. There has been substantial review and due diligence with a variety of professionals, as previously stated.
10. We anticipate the operating expense ratio for the HIRB program to not exceed 1 percent of all liabilities.
11. The ability to meet substantive and compelling political, economic, and social policy objectives without simply mandating the existing broken dysfunctional health financing arena.

12. By design and operation, HIRB program cost less to fund than conventional methods for health financing.

From a budget planning perspective, the costs of funding and paying for health-care services has historically been treated as an annual operating expense. That approach is archaic and is something akin to borrowing for your home in a series of sequential high interest short-term loans, as opposed to consolidating them into a single medium interest long-term mortgage. Continuation of this approach will inevitably lead to (and already has led to) either much higher taxes or significant cuts in benefits—at a time when government faces enormous long-term fiscal challenges and families have experienced decades of stagnant incomes.

The adoption and implementation of the HIRB program will initiate a giant leap toward resolving, restructuring, and creating a state health financing system. It places in alignment the public policy goals of efficient and equitable allocation of resources and is the framework of new allocative and technically efficient streamlined health financing system called the HIRB program.

Frequently Asked Questions

Does HIRB program save money? **Yes**
Based on reasonably conservative parameters, the HIRB program can demonstrate significant real dollar savings (potentially very significant). Of equal importance is the fact that the HIRB program can meet major public policy goals, alleviation of public and private budgetary pressures *without* reducing recipients' benefits and stemming the tide of increased health inflation costs on such budgets.

Does the HIRB program have any downside risk? **No**
If the health inflation rate exceeds that upon which the model is built, more money will need to be contributed into the funding mechanism. The issue is how program adjustments are allocated among the various parties. However, this is not any different than what would occur under any other financing arrangement facing escalating health-care costs.

Most people would consider having to expend more money toward their health care as not good. However ironic, in the HIRB program, the higher the contributions levels, the lower the total funding cost.

In contrast, if the actual health inflation rate is less than that assumed in the financing model, either contribution levels may be reduced or a surplus will accumulate within the funding mechanism. This may allow the existing contributions to remain flat and level for some or all of the parties or possibly even be decreased even with continued medical inflation.

What happens to the HIRB program when interest rates rise?
Interest rates and the prices of outstanding bonds move inversely.

Rising interest rates puts downward pressure on prices of bonds. Decreasing interest rates creates upward pressure on the price of bonds. Neither has any bearing on Bond Issuer. The movement of interest rates, either up or down, only affects the outstanding bondholders.

Relative to the new issuance of new bonds, higher interest rates means higher debt service payments. It also means higher earned interest. It also means the net gain may increase thereby reducing the cost of funding.

CHAPTER 21

HIRB's Versatility

Unless patients pay out of pocket for all their health costs—an unlikely proposal even in libertarian circles—all health policies involve some form of financing. Remember, insurance is a form a financing: one where risks are pooled and costs are spread. In conservative circles, this financing is largely up to private insurers, with the indigent subsidized by general tax revenue. Under progressive plans government takes up a greater financing burden, even undertaking to serve as the insurer under many single payer proposals and some existing programs such as Medicare and Medicaid.

HIRB is an alternative means of financing health care. It works under universal participation, which means mandated participation. It requires an information system to dynamically adjust the HIRB program based on several different variables.

Under the ACA—assuming it survives the 2016 change in government—HIRB can help expand and reduce the cost of funding and alleviate budgetary financial pressures for all parties, public and private:

- Under policies to encourage greater utilization of high deductible health plans such as those of some GOP candidates, HIRB can finance tax credits or similar enrollment incentives.
- Under single payer plans like Sanders', HIRB can finance the increase in government subsidy along the lines previously discussed regarding the ACA.

The foregoing is based on candidates' announced health proposals as this book's writing in fall of 2015.

Beyond Health Care

Although the largest challenge, health-care spending is by no means the only fiscal challenge affecting most governments in the United States. The fiscal system is awash in unsustainable promises founded on faulty demographic assumptions. These have already engendered debt levels previously only seen in wartime. They will soon be aggravated when tens of millions of Baby Boomers are added to the retirement rolls.

A case in point is state and local employee pensions. These defined benefit plans guarantee an income stream for life, premised on investment returns and growing employee contributions that now seem like fantasies. The unfunded portion of state and local retirement systems has accumulated to several trillion dollars—not at the level of the national debt (nearly $20 trillion), but still enough to catch one's breath.

As with health care, these public systems face rapidly escalating liabilities. They can utilize the HIRB approach to leverage these liabilities the way traditional investors leverage ownership of an asset. Key requirements include:

- *Predictable participation.* The beneficiary population must be well known and predictable so that risks can be actuarially forecast with statistical accuracy. This is why most health insurance plans specify universal participation: to avoid adverse selection, where only the sickest join the pool. In many policy areas this is not difficult: Government employers know who their employees are, as the managers of a physical project like a road or a bridge can distinguish paying users. The challenge is political: overcoming libertarian opposition to the exclusion of free riders.
- *Predictable revenue collection.* It must be possible to collect the needed revenue, and to forecast collections in advance to align revenues with costs. Again, for many policy areas this is straightforward: Retirement system payments can be deducted from employee paychecks. Roads and bridges can charge tolls.
- *Open-mindedness about financial innovation.* Political jurisdictions that have seen exotic financial positions blow up on

them (as Orange County, California did in 1994 over index futures, and a number of European towns did over mortgage backed securities in 2008) are unlikely breeding grounds for a new financing approach.

Like any other financing mechanism, the fact that it is feasible does not mean it should automatically be implemented in any given instance. Its viability does not entirely depend on external forces like interest rates or medical inflation: it can break even in a very wide range of circumstances. But its use still requires both enterprise and judgment—qualities not in surplus in American politics.

Disclosures

- Health Insurance Revenue Bonds and HIRB are registered trade or service marks of Randy S. Miller
- If you can't bend the curve on health care cost, then bend the curve on the cost of funding—This is a pending register Trade/Service Mark of Randy S. Miller

HIRB Software is protected by registered copyright. All Rights Reserved.

PART VI

Conclusion

"A politician thinks of the next election. A statesman thinks of the next generation."

—James Freeman Clarke
American theologian and author
(1810–1888)

CHAPTER 22

What Democrats Get Wrong About Health Reform

A large part of real politics is enacting laws that award benefits to constituents, paid for by others. A common error of liberals is to treat health care paid for by government as "free." Somewhat less naïve are those who are for single payer programs based on the asserted efficiencies of Medicare. Finally, many left of center reform proposals attempt to pass costs on to employers, ignoring that they will be passed along to employees.

Single Payer's Limitations

While profit margins among private health insurers are typically in the low double digit range, the Medicare program is often held out as a model of efficiency. Advocates argue that administrative costs consume only a very few percent of total spending. The argument is that the elimination of profits will allow more resources to be directed to actual health care. This logic led to the 2011 enactment of a single payer system in Vermont (later rescinded due to exploding expenses).

The absence of significant competition would seem to remove a major incentive to control costs. So Medicare's efficiency comes as a great surprise. Should it really be a model? There are at least two reasons to be skeptical.

- *Depressed pricing.* For over a decade the rates at which the Medicare program pays health care providers have been well below market prices, averaging less than 80 percent of market for both hospital and doctors' charges, and projected by CBO to fall below 40 percent of market in the coming decades. The difference gets shifted to patient with private insurance,

further escalating premiums. Each year Congress offers partial
relief through a "doc fix" that allows temporarily higher
prices. Nevertheless, in some regions new Medicare patients
cannot be treated because doctors do not accept Medicare
payments. Similar problems are occurring with Medicaid
rolls, now swollen through the Affordable Care Act (ACA).

- *Rationing.* Some medical procedures are not covered by the
program, or are so restricted as to require lengthy waits. This
problem is pervasive in national health care systems in other
countries, as mentioned earlier. Canadians, for instance, end-
run long waits in their national system by paying for private
care in the United States. If patients were spending their
own money, they would ration their demand and buy only
care whose value to them exceeded its cost. This restraint is
nullified by the government subsidy, requiring an alternative
rationing mechanism. All scarce resources are rationed, but
rationing by individual consumers has greater legitimacy than
when undertaken by government functionaries.

It is not surprising therefore that Vermont rescinded its single payer
plan in 2015.

Single payer advocates must meet the burden of showing how their
proposal really achieves its asserted efficiencies. If they can do so, they
must show how single payer can scale up while staying economical.

Problems With Incremental Reforms

As a half measure on the way to a single payer utopia, a number of liberal plans have retained the essential employer-based structure of our
current system. Obama's ACA and the abortive 1993 Hillarycare each
repose primary responsibility for paying for health care with employers.
Firms with more than 50 employees which fail to offer insurance to full
time workers (defined as working at least 30 hours per week) face fines.
(Economists believe this has depressed labor force participation, because
employers have converted some full time jobs to part time, which has
depressed the number of job applicants. Polls by three Federal Reserve

banks have found that between one-fifth and one-third of employers plan to convert some of their fulltime workers to part time in response the ACA mandates.) Individuals who do not have wage employment must purchase health insurance themselves, facing a gradually escalating fine if they fail to do so. These mandates are intended to broaden the risk pool, so that healthy people cross subsidize unhealthy ones. Both Hillarycare and Obamacare required "community rating," in which all members of a demographic group must be charged the same premium. In effect, low risk customers pay for part of high risk customers' insurance.

Although incremental changes to the employer-based system are more centrist than single payer proposals, they merely reallocate expenses rather than stem them. Spending is pushed onto a constituency—employers— that generally leans Republican. Incremental funds to pay for the expansion of Medicaid largely come from GOP constituencies through devices like the surcharge on high income taxpayers.

As noted earlier, Obamacare's widely touted success—reducing the uninsured roles by nearly 10 million people—is unlikely to materially bend the cost curve. Most analyses of recent moderation of health inflation attribute it to economic factors, not policy.

As candidates present their health reform proposals to you, ask yourself questions like these:

- How does the candidate define the core problem? Access challenges are generally a side effect of high costs. Addressing costs will make progress on access.
- What evidence does the candidate offer to support their proposal? Has it been cherry picked, or does it seem representative? Is it on a large enough scale that most negative surprises have been uncovered already?
- If the candidate claims their reforms will lower health care costs, examine the accounting carefully. Many claimed savings are simply accounting reallocations.

CHAPTER 23

What Republicans Get Wrong About Health Reform

GOP health positions are less diverse than Democrats'. There are two main types:

- *Reflexive repealers.* As noted in Chapter 8, a number of leading GOP figures have staked their political futures on the repeal of the ACA. Several of them have not made a specific proposal for replacing it. While we are no fans of Obamacare, we consider it irresponsible for a candidate's entire health reform platform to be the word "No."
- *Free market fanboys.* Many conservatives are so enamored of the free market that they fail to check to see how free a given real market actually is. Chapter 11 identifies a number of forces combine to push American health care very far from the ideal of "perfect competition."

Several GOP presidential candidates appear to be reflexive repealers, as befits sitting legislators who may eventually face serious bills to repeal or gut the ACA. In the jockeying to "out-conservative" the field in the primary campaign, many others are making free market fanboy noises.

Elements of Progress

One of the more positive developments of the past decade has been tax legislation to encourage new insurance arrangements that are truly insurance. With auto insurance, the policyholder is paid only if they suffer an accident. But health insurance covers a very wide range of medical expenses, including the equivalent of oil changes and refueling. Although deductibles and copayment requirements attempted to expose patients to financial impacts from their care decisions, other peoples' money still paid for the vast majority of an individual's medical costs. HMOs and other innovations of the late 20th century, where providers were paid a fixed amount (a "capitated," or per capita, rate) per patient, were coping mechanisms that failed to overcome the fundamental weaknesses of third party payment.

Beginning in the mid-1990s and expanded in the 2000s, a new type of plan was authorized by Congress that has offered some mild relief. Known under the marketing spin of "consumer driven health plans," their more descriptive name is high deductible health plans. Typically, patients are responsible for the first $1,000+ of medical expenses in a given year. Insurance coverage effectively begins thereafter, with the insurer paying the vast majority of expenses above the deductible and the patient some-times responsible for a minority (e.g., 10 percent). This restores health insurance to its true insurance purpose: to financially protect against serious illness.

Not surprisingly, employers have embraced consumer driven plans, because premiums are far lower. Many employers offer incentives to encourage employees to switch to these plans; an increasing number of firms offer only this type. Enrollment has mushroomed from almost no one a decade ago to about 15 million enrollees today.

A fair concern about these plans is that consumers will stint on routine care. We are not concerned about how many toasters or video games a household buys; nor should we be about their health-care purchases, with two exceptions.

First, some employed heads of households will eventually become indigent and become eligible for publically paid care such as Medicaid. Inadequate care while they were working may aggravate conditions that will be treated later (and paid for by taxpayers) when they are indigent.

Second, treatable communicable diseases may spread more rapidly if the carrier fails to get treatment because of excessive frugality. In public health, no patient is an island.

These concerns suggest a need to refine the high deductible idea, not reject it. Certain preventive treatments could be exempt from the deductible, or subject to a lower copayment requirement. Of course, any implicit subsidy of certain treatments will create an incentive to over-diagnose illnesses eligible for those treatments.

Unfairness in Tax Subsidies

Only a few brave Republicans have pointed out that the federal bias toward employer-sponsored health insurance is deeply regressive: The value of the tax deduction of insurance on families with incomes over $150,000 is twenty times that of insurance on families that earn one tenth as much. This is inevitable given the United States' progressive income tax structure: a given deduction is worth far more to a household paying a relatively high tax rate. Conservatives should be in the forefront of efforts to equalize health insurance's tax treatment regardless of employment status or income. The ACA ignored this.

The Truly Indigent

This discussion of preventive care is especially pertinent to indigent care. Poor people have a higher incidence of chronic illnesses—often those illnesses contributed to their impoverishment. If they cannot afford routine medical care, in desperate situations they often fall back on the facilities legally mandated to treat them. Unfortunately, those facilities are also the most expensive locations to receive primary care: emergency rooms. Although cost reduction was not a significant emphasis of Obamacare, it may achieve some savings to the degree that expanded insurance reduces emergency room visits.

Even leaving aside charity or sympathy, assurance of some level of basic care is a public health imperative. The challenge, as so often in politics, is balancing individual freedom with public welfare. But protecting public health need not mean full public funding. There is a strong argument that all beneficiaries of public subsidies should make a partial contribution to the benefit they receive. Otherwise there is no governor on demand, and society bifurcates into a receiving and providing class, which is corrosive to democracy.

CHAPTER 24

The Path to a Sustainable Health System

"Today's problems were yesterday's solutions."
—former Senator Sam Nunn (D, Georgia)

America's health-care system is like a termite-infested house kept standing by ever-thicker layers of paint. The industry is very far from the competitive Nirvana beloved of economists and conservatives. But proposals to correct it by discarding market principles in favor of government can spark a cure even worse than the disease.

Candidates jockeying to recruit their partisan bases regularly spout platitudes that ignore the dysfunctional realities. Liberals don't acknowledge the limitations of publicly financed benefits. Conservatives assume a competitive landscape that does not exist. This book provides some principles for more productive reform.

But until the day when genuine health reform is enacted, how can we pay for the system we have? This book also describes an approach. It can be profitably implemented by any entity that takes financial responsibility for the care of a defined population (program beneficiaries, or company employees). It can be implemented by public or private organizations. And it leverages health inflation to make it an asset, not a liability. Part V describes this approach: the Health Insurance Revenue Bond (HIRB®). We illustrated HIRB® as issued by a state, because we believe it has great promise for U.S. states. But it is adaptable by almost any issuer to finance its health-care obligations, including private employers who cover employees, or nonprofit coops authorized and subsidized by the ACA.

HIRB generates the working capital to finance any system reform that will make a health program fiscally sustainable. As noted, its basic purpose is similar to any refinancing: using that working capital to convert a rapidly escalating liability (like a high interest mortgage) into a more sustainable one.

Not all states' fiscal and political climates are ripe for HIRB. The conditions that are most promising for success include:

- *A below-average level of outstanding debt.* Governments groaning under the weight of accumulated past debts will have extremely limited appetite for new debt, regardless of its financial advantages. So, the most promising population of states that might be early HIRB adopters will probably be limited to those with a lower debt burden. But if after issuance a state wished to terminate the HIRB financing strategy, in any given month there are sufficient assets to pay all benefit liabilities accrued to date as well as allow for redemption, all the outstanding bonds. There are no unfunded liabilities to program beneficiaries or bondholders. *Note: This issue is strictly symbolic and political, not substantive, since HIRB® is designed as a self-liquidating revenue bond that should not impinge the state's overall fiscal position.*
- *Recent successes with financial innovation.* HIRB will receive the warmest welcome in a jurisdiction that has recently used an innovation like a refinancing to achieve some widely recognized fiscal success. This is most promising if that success was quite recent, like within the last one or two election cycles. Political memories are exceptionally short.
- *Program reform proposals with substantial support.* Each state doubtless has a number of unsustainable program obligations, and proposals for reform. We have outlined several in this book. HIRB has the best chance to succeed when the primary obstacle to implementing reform is the hurdle of transition costs. The transition costs currently preoccupying health officials are those to implement the ACA, but nearly every reform requires short run expenditures to achieve longer term benefits.

This novel financing approach draws from several disciplines that do not normally intersect, including public finance, insurance, and health policy. Organizations interested in issuing such bonds need to be discriminating in their choice of advisers. A multidisciplinary perspective is essential.

No Long Bombs

As Part II made abundantly clear, we have not been well served by grand schemes to remake the health-care system. Any sector that consumes nearly 20 percent of GDP has a vast number of moving parts, and it is disingenuous to suggest that we can predict how they all will react to a systemic change. Unfortunately, many bold changes have ignored the termite-infested foundation and simply added more layers of paint.

Health reform is a game of inches gained in short runs, not by long bomb passes. The ACA may well have preempted further reforms at the national level for several election cycles. For the meantime, the locus of innovation is likely to be in states and among private employers. But while we wait, our system's finances need repair. Financial innovations like HIRB, which transcend ideology, are a sensible interim step.

Glossary

ACA (Affordable Care Act): Short name for the Patient Protection and Affordable Care Act (often known colloquially as "Obamacare") signed into law in 2010. Highly controversial and passed on a pure party line vote in Congress, it has survived two Supreme Court challenges as of the summer of 2015.

Advance prefunding: See **Prefunding**.

Adverse selection: Self-selection by the riskiest members of a population to purchase insurance. In the extreme, people could wait until symptoms appeared before they enrolled in health insurance. Adverse selection—a riskier-then-expected policyholder population—is often behind surprise spikes in insurance premiums. Avoiding adverse selection was the stated goal behind many insurers' exclusion from coverage of prior medical conditions. Adverse selection is avoided under **universal coverage**.

Arbitrage: The act of buying and selling the same item in two different markets or at two different times, to profit from any price difference (the "arbitrage spread.") Banks' primary business is arbitrage: borrowing money at low rates and lending at higher rates.

Arbitrage Bonds are bonds issued by a government unit in order to gain an interest rate advantage by refunding higher-rate bonds in advance of their call date. Proceeds from the lower-rate refunded issue are invested in U.S. Treasuries securities until the first call of the higher-rate bond issue being refunded, such as an **Advance Refunding**. Any realized arbitrage profit related to tax-exempt bonds must be rebated to the federal government.

Asset: Any item that generates an income. Assets can be real, such as property; or financial, such as stocks or bonds.

Baby Boom: Americans born between 1946 and 1964, a very large demographic cohort (roughly 80 million individuals). Their numbers have driven large parts of the economy throughout their lives. As they now begin to retire, their claims on retiree entitlement programs like Social Security and Medicare will further aggravate government **fiscal** challenges; members of the cohort are called **Boomers**.

Baseline model: This is a HIRB financing model developed from demographic profile and other data on the covered population. It is used to dynamically manage the HIRB program. Examples of output of a baseline model are in Chapter 18.

Basis point: One one-hundredth of one percent. So 0.50 percent (1/2 of 1 percent) is 50 basis points, often abbreviated as "50 bps."

Bending the cost curve: See **cost curve**.

Benefits, health: the commitment made by insurers to pay all or part of medical expenses in accordance with a health insurance contract. These are enumerated in a **schedule of benefits**, which can vary by insurer. Traditionally, any mandates on benefits have been imposed by states, although some were included in ACA.

Bonds: Bonds are debt instruments. Bond issuers borrow funds from bond investors (purchasers) and commit to repay the principal and interest on an agreed schedule. Municipal bonds are issued by governments, and enjoy favorable tax treatment (interest payments are not taxable to the bondholder) if they qualify for tax exempt status. **HIRB** is a type of muni bond, although it can also be used by taxable issuers.

Bonds, general obligation (G.O.): Bonds secured by the full faith and credit of the issuer. In theory governments can draw from any revenue source, including raising taxes, to service G.O. bonds. See also **G.O.**

Bond Rate: The rate of interest rate paid on the bond.

Bonds, revenue: Bonds secured by revenues from the project being financed. Revenue bonds are commonly used for projects that have an organic revenue stream, such as a toll road, that can service the bond.

Bonds, tax-exempt: Interest in some bonds are exempt from federal taxes, and may be exempt from state taxes. See **municipal bonds**.

Bond Underwriter(s): A company or other entity that administers the public issuance and distribution of securities from a corporation or government issuing body. The Underwriter(s) buys the entire bond issue from the Issuer and then sells them to investors.

Boomers: Members of the Bab Boom generation. In 2015, Boomers were between 51 and 69 years old.

Cadillac tax: A provision of the ACA that imposes a tax surcharge on especially generous health insurance policies, which will go into effect in 2018. The fiscal rationale for this tax is that it helped defray part of the cost of the ACA's expansion. The policy objective is to discourage overutilization of health care. Since generous benefits are a core goal of many labor unions (a base Democratic constituency), several Democratic candidates have denounced the tax or suggested revisions.

Callable Bonds are bonds that can be redeemed prior to the stated maturity. This is referenced as **Early Bond Redemption**.

Capitated or capitation: Payment of medical providers per patient head (per capita), a model which significantly supplanted "**fee for service**" payments (reimburse for each specific service) by insurance companies. Capitation models shifted risk from insurers to providers, and are intended to encourage increased provider efficiency. Critics argue that capitation encourages stinting on necessary care.

Cartel is an organization created from agreement (formal or implicit) among a group of producers of a good or service, to regulate supply in an effort to manipulate (raise) prices.

Community rating: The setting of insurance premium rates identically for all members of a "community," such as all members of a group such as the employees of the same firm. This precludes setting premiums based on an individual's level of risk. It is a feature of the ACA, as it was of the aborted **Health Security Act** of 1993 to 1994.

Consolidation of an industry: The process by which the number of competitors shrinks, by mergers or by firm failure. A more consolidated industry usually means less competition and higher prices.

Consumer-driven health plans: See **high deductible health plans**.

Consumer Price Index (CPI): A measure, tabulated by the Bureau of Labor Statistics, of prices. It combines a variety of goods and purchased by urban consumers, weighted in proportion to their purchases. Annual change in the CPI is the generally-accepted measure of **inflation**. A number of CPIs are computed for different types of consumers, and for different sectors of the economy.

Copay: A percentage of the price of a medical procedure for which the patient is responsible, after their **deductible** has been met. If for example a patient's policy has a $1,000 annual deductible, they are responsible for all payments up to that amount. If thereafter their copay is 10 percent, they will be responsible for 10 percent of all bills above $1,000. In this illustration, if their total medical bills for the year were $3,000, they would be responsible for $1,200: $1,000 in deductible and (10% × $2,000) in copays.

Cost Curve refers to the trend in health-care spending over time, usually shown as a line graph. For most of the past several decades, spending has risen at several times the rate of general economic growth or the Consumer Price Index (CPI). "Bending the cost curve" generally means slowing the rate of growth in health spending.

Covered risk or event: Something on an insurers' list of events that they have agreed to reimburse under the terms of their contract with the policyholder.

Deductible: Most insurance policies only pay claims after the policyholder has absorbed the "deductible" loss—the insurer *deducts* this amount before making payment. As with **copays**, the purpose is to limit **moral hazard** (see) by exposing the policyholder to partial loss, to discourage fraudulent or frivolous claims.

Deferred Health Maintenance Costs refers to the anticipated yet unknown costs incurred from those who deferred health care for a variety of reasons, now seek treatment and causing of flood of demand driving a spike in costs.

Discretionary programs: Government spending programs for which spending can be reset each year.

Early Bond Redemption: see **Callable bonds**.

Entitlement programs: Government programs for which eligibility is automatic and spending is legally mandated: that is, where the program beneficiaries are "entitled" to benefits. Examples are: Social Security (retirement income); Medicare (retiree health care); and unemployment insurance (temporary income replacement for the involuntarily unemployed). As long as the program remains authorized, any eligible beneficiary must be paid. This contrasts with government **discretionary** programs.

ERISA: Employee retirement and Income Security Act, a federal law passed in 1974. EIRSA governs employee pensions and retirement plans, but it also governs employer self-funded health benefit plans, exempting them from the jurisdiction of state insurance commissioners that applies to all traditional health insurers.

Fee for service: An insurance payment approach that reimburses providers for each specific service performed. Critics argue that it has encouraged excessive treatment.

FFP (Federal Financial Participation): This is the name of the annual expenditures the federal government pays for Medicaid in a particular state. The minimum FFP is 50 percent of the Medicaid health care cost.

Fiscal: Pertaining to spending and revenue, that is, spending and revenues.

G.O.—General Obligation Bonds are bonds issued by a State or a political subdivision. The security for the bonds is the Bond Issuer's authority to levy taxes sufficient to pay the principal and interest due on the bonds when payable.

Guaranteed issue: A commitment by an insurer to offer a policy regardless of the individual policyholder's riskiness. In contrast, **underwriting** entails evaluating an applicant's risk level, to decide whether or not to offer coverage. Employment-based coverage is typically less expensive than individual coverage because premium levels are based on the average riskiness of all employees. Any employee of a firm which has secured a group policy is guaranteed issue of a policy.

Health Security Act: Legislation proposed by the Clinton Administration in late 1993, developed by a White House task force chaired by then-First Lady Hillary Clinton. Subjected to intense opposition by the insurance industry, it failed Senate passage in 1994.

High deductible health plan (HDHPs): An insurance plan that only begins reimbursing policyholders after a larger-than-usual deductible, typically several thousand dollars. The premise is that patients will be more careful consumers if more of their own money is in play. Uptake of these plans has been significant, driven by tax benefits, and by employers' incentives to encourage employees to enroll. Also known as **consumer-driven health plans**.

Health Insurance Revenue Bond® and its acronym **HIRB**®: Health Insurance Revenue Bond, a proposed advance prefunded debt instrument to pay a calculated stream of health care liabilities, developed by Randy S. Miller (this book's coauthor). See Part V.

(Trust) **Indenture** is an agreement between a bond issuer and a trustee, representing the bondholder's interests and the rules and responsibilities that each party must adhere to.

Inflation: The change in level of prices from one year to the next. General price level changes are reflected in the **Consumer price index (CPI)**. There are also more sector-specific inflation measures, such as medical inflation, which has far outpaced the CPI.

Insurance: A commitment by a financial organization to pay its policy-holder if a covered event (a death, a fire, or illness) occurs. The policy-holder pays premiums to the insurer. The insurer charges an amount that, combined across all policyholders, will be sufficient to pay the predicted number of claims. Claim experience is more predictable if the pool of policyholders is large. In essence, insurance is a means of financing.

Insurance Underwriting is a quality control process whereby an insurer gathers personal, financial, medical, and other information on a prospective insured to determine if the insured is an acceptable risk and to rate the premium for the insured's health coverage.

Insurer's Obligations: All outstanding policy liabilities (benefits to policyholders) of an insurer.

Leverage: Borrowing money to achieve a financial objective. Assets are often bought with leverage (e.g., a home mortgage). **HIRB** is a strategy to leverage liabilities.

Liability is a claim on assets, excluding ownership equity of a company or individual. It represents a transfer of assets or services on a specified date. The event that created the obligation has already occurred. The company or individual has no option to avoid the transfer.

Mandate (to purchase health insurance): To assure that a risk pool's level of risk can be predicted, all members of that population may be mandated to enroll in coverage. This **universal coverage** requirement is opposed by those who believe in maximum individual freedom.

Medical loss ratio (MLR): The percentage of an insurer's premium revenues paid out in claims. Roughly speaking, (1 − MLR) is the insurer's profit margin.

Moral hazard: The expectation that a safety net (like insurance) will encourage risky behavior. This was a pervasive issue when major banks self-sabotaged in the 2008 financial crisis; it comes up (though less often) regarding insurance-covered events.

Municipal bonds: "Munis" are bonds issued by state and local governments. Most of the interest they pay is not taxed at the federal level (to encourage purchasers to buy the bonds); most are also exempt from state taxes if the purchaser is a resident of the state where it was issued.

Obamacare: See **ACA (Affordable Care Act)**.

Project: Specifically in the context of HIRB program it is the design, development, construction, and operation of an integrated financial information management system that will operate, manage, and administer the HIRB program.

Prefunding: Placing funds in escrow to assure that bondholders will be paid on time. Prefunding enhances the quality of a credit so as to lower its interest rate.

Risk pool: A population from whom an insurer collects premiums which collectively pay to reimburse members who experience a **covered event**. While the odds of an event occurring for an individual are difficult to estimate, their incidence can be predicted quite accurately over a large population. So larger risk pools typically experience fewer surprises and unexpected losses (where reimbursements exceed premium income).

Savings or Gains: The difference between health-care expenditures made under present financing schemes versus the amount of expenditures made under the HIRB program.

Schedule of benefits: The specification by an insurance company of what its policy covers: events, deductibles, and maximum payments. This is part of an insurance policy contract.

Single payer: A medical payment system in which a single entity—usually government or a quasigovernmental organization—pays for members' health expenses. This contrasts with a competitive payment system in which multiple payers—usually insurance companies—compete for the right to pay for the health care of members and collect premiums from those members.

Third-party payment: Medical payment systems in which a patient makes care choices (advised by their doctor), but the costs are mostly paid by others. In the United States, employees of firms which offer insurance will have most of their medical costs paid by insurers contracted by their employers. Senior citizens will select care paid for mostly be the Medicare program. In such situations where the key decision maker does not bear much of the financial costs of the decision, it can be argued this incentivizes overuse of care.

Underwriting: An insurer's quality control process to evaluate an applicant's risk level, to decide whether or not to offer coverage. **Guaranteed issue** to a group essentially prohibits underwriting for members of that group.

Universal coverage: A system in which all members of a population are covered by insurance, to avoid **adverse selection**. Achieving this typically requires **mandates**.

Notes

Chapter 14

1. McKinsey Global Institute Study, Debt & Deleveraging, February 2015.

Chapter 16

1. Gottret and Schieber (2006, 4–5).
2. Gottret and Schieber (2006, 2).
3. Gottret and Schieber (2006, 5–6).
4. Gottret and Schieber (2006, 6).
5. Gottret and Schieber (2006, 7–12).

Chapter 17

1. Scaer (2005).

Bibliography

Associated Press. August 1, 2015. "Health Law's Nonprofit Insurance Co-Ops Awash in Red Ink."

Barr, D. 2011. *Introduction to US Health Policy.* Baltimore, MD: Johns Hopkins University Press.

Bell, K. August 27, 2015. "Could Obamacare's Cadillac Tax Kill FSAs?" *Bankrate.*

Blumenthal, D., K. Davis, and S. Guterman. January 29, 2015. "Medicare at 50—Origins and Evolution." *New England Journal of Medicine* 372, no. 5, pp. 479–86.

Blumenthal, D., and W. Hsiao. April 2, 2015. "Lessons from the East—China's Rapidly Evolving Health Care System." *New England Journal of Medicine* 372, no. 14, pp. 1281–85.

Blumenthal, D., and J.A. Morone. 2010. *The Heart of Power: Health and Politics in the Oval Office.* Berkeley, CA: University of California Press.

Blumenthal, D., K. Stremikis, and D. Cutler. December 26, 2013. "Health Care Spending—A Giant Slain or Sleeping?" *New England Journal of Medicine* 369, no. 26, pp. 2551–57.

Claxton, G., and L. Lavitt. August 25, 2015. "How Many Employers Could Be Affected by the Cadillac Plan Tax?" Kaiser Family Foundation.

Clinton, H.R. 2014. "Now Can We Talk About Health Care?" *New York Times Magazine*, April 18.

Cogan, J.F., R.G. Hubbard, and D.P. Kessler. 2005. *Healthy, Wealthy and Wise: Five Steps to a Better Health Care System.* Washington, DC: AEI Press.

Evans, R. 1984. *Strained Mercy: The Economics of Canadian Health Care.* Toronto: Butterworth-Heinemann.

Frum, D. 2015. "The Question that Will Decide the 2016 Election." *The Atlantic*, April 22.

Goodman, J.C. 2014. *A Better Choice: Healthcare Solutions for America.* Independent Institute.

Greenberg, S. 2015. "Stephan Seiler: Can Hospital Competition Save Lives?" *Stanford Business*, June 28.

Gottret, P., and G. Schieber. 2006. *Health Financing Revisited—A Practitioner's Guide.* The International Bank for Reconstruction and Development/The World Bank.

Gutierrez, C., and U. Ranji. 2003. "U.S. Health Care Costs Background Brief," "National Health Expenditures," "What Is Driving Health Care Costs?" KaiserEd u.org (Updated September 2005).

Hoffman, B. 2012. *Health Care for Some: Rights and Rationing in the United States Since 1930.* Chicago, IL: University of Chicago Press.

Jacobs, L.R., and T. Skocpol. 2012. *Health Care Reform and American Politics.* Oxford, UK: Oxford University Press.

Levitt, L., G. Claxton, and C. Cox. June 1, 2015. "How Have Insurers Fared Under the Affordable Care Act?" Kaiser Family Foundation. http://kff.org/private-insurance/perspective/how-have-insurers-fared-under-the-affordable-care-act/

McClaughry, J. 2014. "The First Single Payer Domino." *National Review*, July 15.

McKinsey Global Institute Study. February 2015. "Debt & Deleveraging."

McLaughlin, D. April 3, 2014. "Yes, There's A Republican Health Care Plan: Bobby Jindal's Plan." The Hill.

Nather, D. 2014. "Health Care Wonks Turn to 2016." *Politico*, April 26.

Pipes, S. 2004. *Miracle Cure: How to Solve America's Healthcare Crisis and Why Canada Isn't the Answer.* Pacific Research Institute.

Porter, M.E., and E.O. Teisberg. 2006. *Redefining Health Care: Value-Based Competition on Results.* Cambridge, MA: Harvard Business School Press.

Rosin, T., K. Gooch, and E. Rappleye. 2015. "2016 Presidential Viewpoint: 44 Views on Healthcare from Bush, Carson, Rubio, Paul, Clinton." *Becker's Hospital Review*, June 23.

Rubio, M. 2015. "My Plan to Fix Health Care." *Politico*, August 17.

Scaer, R.C. 2005. *The Trauma Spectrum: Hidden Wounds and Human Resiliency.* New York: W. W. Norton & Company.

Scott Walker for President. April 2015. "The Day One Patient Freedom Plan."

Shultz, G.P., and J.B. Shoven. 2008. *Putting Our House in Order: A Guide to Social Security and Health Care Reform.* New York: W. W. Norton & Company.

Starr, P. 1983. *The Social Transformation of American Medicine.* New York: Basic Books.

Starr, P. 2007. "The Hillarycare Mythology." *American Prospect*, September 13.

Starr, P. 2011. *Remedy and Reaction: The Peculiar American Struggle Over Health Care Reform.* New Haven, CT: Yale University Press.

Toner, R., and A.E. Kornblut. 2006. "Wounds Salved, Clinton Returns to Health Care." *New York Times*, June 10.

Viebeck, E. August 17, 2013. "Many 2016 Republican Presidential Hopefuls Agree: Defund ObamaCare." The Hill.

Wall Street Journal. 2015. "The Post-ObamaCare Debate Begins." August 19.

For More About HIRB

The Health Insurance Revenue Bond™ (HIRB™) was invented by Randy S. Miller. It allows a state to finance reforms to their health-care systems, providing working capital needed to pay transition costs. It exploits health inflation to leverage a financial liability, analogous to investors who commonly leverage the ownership of an asset. It can be used by any jurisdiction with a public financed health program, or a firm that funds employee or retiree health care.

HIRB has undergone extensive due diligence by several states. Its structure has been extended to a range of public financings.

The authors can be available to assist organizations interested in issuing HIRB bonds.

Further details on HIRB, including an owner's manual for prospective issuers, is available from the authors at: suigenerishirb@gmail.com.

Index

OTHER TITLES FROM THE ECONOMICS COLLECTION

Philip Romero, The University of Oregon and
Jeffrey Edwards, North Carolina A&T State University, Editors

- *The Economics of Civil and Common Law* by Zagros Madjd-Sadjadi
- *Leveraging Cultural Diversity in Emerging Markets* by Marcus Goncalves and Finn Majlergaard
- *Business Liability and Economic Damages* by Scott Gilbert
- *Seeing the Future: How to Build Basic Forecasting Models* by Tam Bang Vu
- *U.S. Politics and the American Macroeconomy* by Gerald T. Fox
- *Global Public Health Policies: Case Studies from India on Planning and Implementation* by KV Ramani
- *How Strong is Your Firm's Competitive Advantage, Second Edition* by Daniel Marburger
- *Statistics for Economics, Second Edition* by Shahdad Naghshpour
- *Regression for Economics, Second Edition* by Shahdad Naghshpour
- *Eastern European Economies: A Region in Transition* by Marcus Goncalves and Erika Cornelius Smith

Announcing the Business Expert Press Digital Library

Concise e-books business students need for classroom and research

This book can also be purchased in an e-book collection by your library as

- a one-time purchase,
- that is owned forever,
- allows for simultaneous readers,
- has no restrictions on printing, and
- can be downloaded as PDFs from within the library community.

Our digital library collections are a great solution to beat the rising cost of textbooks. E-books can be loaded into their course management systems or onto students' e-book readers.
The **Business Expert Press** digital libraries are very affordable, with no obligation to buy in future years. For more information, please visit **www.businessexpertpress.com/librarians**. To set up a trial in the United States, please email **sales@businessexpertpress.com**.

www.ingramcontent.com/pod-product-compliance
Lightning Source LLC
Chambersburg PA
CBHW062013200326
41519CB00017B/4791